The Tomás Cruz Conga Method

VOLUME III • ADVANCED

Timba: Modern Cuban Conga Rhythms

by **Tomás Cruz**
with Kevin Moore,
Mike Gerald and Orlando Fiol

Online Video www.melbay.com/20301MEB

Cover Design: Bill Wolfer bill@mamborama.com
Recording studio photos: Tom Ehrlich tjejazz@sbcglobal.net
DVD Recorded at: Little Gypsy Studios, Santa Cruz, CA
Skin on Skin Congas provided by: Javier Muñiz

MEL BAY ®

1 2 3 4 5 6 7 8 9 0

Visit us on the Web at www.melbay.com — E-mail us at email@melbay.com

Table of Contents

PART 3: LEARNING TIMBA MARCHAS

PART 4: TIMBA MARCHAS WITH STEP BY STEP VIDEO TRAINING

Marchas from Tomasito's recordings with Paulito FG:

Marchas from Recordings with El Médico de la Salsa:

PART 5: LONGER MARCHAS

Longer Marchas from Recordings with Paulito FG:

PART 7: ANALYSIS OF A COMPLETE TIMBA ARRANGEMENT

PART 8: INVENTING YOUR OWN CONGA PARTS

PART 9: EXERCISES IN 8TH NOTES 64

Preface

The Mystery of Modern Cuban Conga Playing

Most congueros, whether students or professionals, quickly find themselves on an emotional roller coaster when they first go to Cuba or to hear a modern Cuban band on tour. It begins with shock – the level of musicianship, even among 12 and 13 year old kids, is astounding. Shock gives way to euphoria as the newcomer realizes that he or she has just stumbled on perhaps the most creative chapter in the history of Latin music. Euphoria gives way to a determination to learn this new style, and finally, confusion and frustration reign supreme! Latin percussion usually involves learning a different set of fairly strict rhythmic patterns for each style, but what patterns are these Cubans using? The groove is overwhelming, but the conguero almost seems to be improvising. It's hard to pick out the pattern because it keeps changing, and the same problems come up when trying to analyze the patterns of the drums, timbales, bongó, bass and piano.

The next step, of course, is to seek help, but the vast majority of teachers and methods, both inside and outside of Cuba, begin by teaching basic historical rhythms and never seem to get to what's actually being played in today's Cuban concerts. And most videos and method books by famous virtuoso congueros tend to focus on soloing or pedagogic exercises rather than the actual content of the recordings and concerts which inspired the student's interest in the first place. The magical groove of the modern Cuban rhythm section remains a mystery.

Solving the Mystery – The Story of the Tomás Cruz DVD Method

We were determined not to let these books fall into the same traps as their predecessors, so to ensure we'd get to the final goal, we started at the end and worked backwards. We tackled Volume III first, immersing ourselves in the real music that's being played in the nightclubs and concert halls of Havana today – the music of the leading bands of Cuba – Paulito FG, Manolín (El Médico de la Salsa), Los Van Van, NG La Banda, Bamboleo, Klimax, Issac Delgado, Manolito y su Trabuco, Charanga Habanera, Carlos Manuel, Azúcar Negra, etc. As anyone who's heard these bands live will testify, you can study Mambo, Guaracha and Salsa for a lifetime and still have no idea whatsoever what the congueros are doing in this type of music!

So our first step was to find one of the leading congueros of the modern Cuban style and we were lucky enough to discover that our dream candidate had recently moved to Miami and was willing to take on the project. Tomás "Tomasito" Cruz grew up in the middle of the musical revolution that took place in Havana in the 90's. It was he who invented and performed the ground-breaking conga parts on perhaps the greatest Timba album ever recorded, Paulito FG's "Con la conciencia tranquila". After relocating to Miami in 1998, he joined another of the leading Timba bands, "Manolín, El Médico de la Salsa". He also plays with top traditional Latin artists such as Celia Cruz and Willie Chirino.

The second step was to cut through the verbiage and ask Tomás to demonstrate *exactly* what he plays, all the way through, on specific songs from Paulito FG's legendary "Con la conciencia tranquila" and various Timba classics from Tomasito's current group, "El Médico de la Salsa". We videotaped him playing along with his own recordings and then asked him to study the video footage, explain his approach, analyze the arrangement as a whole, and isolate key patterns and techniques. For each rhythm taught in Volume III, we tell you exactly where to find it on a specific recording. These are not "etudes" or exercises invented for the sake of writing a method book – this is the real deal.

The next task was to present the rhythms in such a simple way that readers would be able to learn them quickly and without frustration – not just watch the DVD once and then file it away with the other method books for future reference. We created a simple and clear notation system which combines standard rhythmic notation with easy to understand letters which can be easily read by those who don't read music, and then we went a step further by inventing the **Step by Step DVD Method**, which makes it fast and easy to learn the patterns without even looking at the book. An equally important advantage of the DVD method is that, instead of spending time trying to decipher printed notation, all of the student's practice time is spent in rhythm, watching one of the world's funkiest congueros and absorbing the intangible nuances of his technique and body language.

Satisfied that Volume III had accomplished its goal, we began Volume II, which covers the roots of Timba – the Cuban, Afro-Cuban and non-Cuban rhythms invented prior to 1990 which formed the rhythmic vocabulary of the Timba pioneers – rhythms such as Songo, Mozambique, Bomba, Guaguancó, 6/8, etc. Volume II also uses the Step by Step DVD Method, but the rhythms are considerably easier. Like Volume III, Volume II gives you the music history to go with the patterns and identifies classic recordings on which they can be found.

Finally, we wrote Volume I, in which Tomasito reveals the time-tested conga method which he himself studied with Changuito and other master congueros at the ENA conservatory in Havana. Volume I starts at the absolute beginning and is designed for the person who has never touched the congas, but is also of great value to the advanced player who wishes to understand the foundation and rudiments of the approach that has allowed the ENA and the other Havana conservatories to consistently turn out so many world-class congueros each year. Volume I begins with simple exercises to develop technique and systematically works its way to basic rhythm patterns such as Salsa, Cha Cha and Bolero, which are presented using the Step by Step DVD method. It also contains an extensive series of rudiments and "recursos" for use in solos and fills. This is continued in Volume II.

The Tomás Cruz Conga Method
Volume I - Beginning
Conga Technique as Taught in Cuba
Mel Bay Catalog #20299DP

The Tomás Cruz Conga Method
Volume II - Intermediate
Essential Conga Rhythms
Mel Bay Catalog #20300DP

ACKNOWLEDGEMENTS

Tomás Cruz: Este libro es el resultado de mucho estudio, sacrificio y dedicación, el mismo no se pudiera haber escrito sin la ayuda de muchas personas, a las cuales quiero darles mi agradecimiento.

Tuve mis primeros estudios en la E.V.A. (Escuela Vocacional de Arte) en Pinar del Río, Cuba, donde mis maestros fueron muy estrictos y grandiosos (Gilberto, Tomas Torre, Néstor Luis y Héctor). También quiero agradecer a mis maestros de solfeo, historia de la música, piano, etc.

A mis grandes amigos y compañeros de estudios de mi año (Omar Rojas, Ciro Parlá, Eddie Pérez, Jorge Castillo, Iván González, Iliana Castillo, Ademilis Hernández) que fueron consejeros y compañía en mi vida.

Vale reconocer la presencia de una persona, a la cual yo quiero y admiro mucho: José Luis Quintana (Changuito) por haberme enseñado la belleza, la técnica y la magia de la Conga. Junto a mí, otros estudiantes como Yoel del Sol, Carlos Reyes, Pedro Pablo Martínez, que tuvieron la suerte de haber aprendido este estilo maravilloso.

También quiero mencionar a una persona muy especial en mi vida (Adolfo Orta, mi maestro de trombón, que mas bien no fue maestro, fue un amigo). Quiero darle las gracias a mi maestro de Batá, Nardo (el Gollo) que me dió la posibilidad de aprender un instrumento tan lindo y rico en ritmo, el cual me ayudó y me dio capacidad en mi mente para mezclar y combinar ritmo de Batá con la Conga.

Es muy importante señalar mis compañeros de banda, Yoel Páez, Yoel Domínguez, Sergio Noroña, Fran Rubio, Yosvel Bernal, Alexander Abreu, Joaquín Díaz, Carlos Pérez, Juan Manuel Ceruto, por haberme ayudado a enriquecer mi mente de su sabiduría.

Quiero hablar sobre la persona más importante en el proceso de este libro, una persona de una inteligencia genial, a la cual le doy las gracias por ser el creador de la idea para hacer este libro: Kevin Moore. Además, agradecer a Mike Gerald por haber dedicado parte de su tiempo para escribir muy rápidamente este método de percusión, y gracias a Orlando Fiol por habernos aconsejado y ayudado con su gran experiencia en la cración de este libro.

Me gustaría mencionar en este agradecimiento los congueros, que fueron mis patrones a seguir: Jorge Alfonso (El Niño) y Angá (Irakere), Andrés Miranda (Negrón), Tomás Ramos, Juan Nogueras (Wickly), Tata Güines, los Papines, el Goyo (maestro del I.S.A.), José Luis Quintana (Changuito), Manolo (Van Van), Yulo (N.G. La Banda), Yoel Drigs, etc.

También quiero darle las gracias a timba.com, Duniel Deya, y a mi gente de California que me ayudaron en mi estancia allá: Michel, Johann, Alexis, Alain, Fito, Bárbara, Javier, Osvaldo, y Joanna.

Espero que este diferente y nuevo método ayude a todos los congueros a desarrollar la técnica de Timba de una manera rápida y eficaz para que el mundo cuente con buenos congueros.

English translation by Tanja Cruz: This book is the result of many years of studies, sacrifice and dedication and could not have been written without the support of many individuals, whom I would like to acknowledge.

My first studies took place at the E.V.A. Vocational School of Arts (Escuela Vocacional de Arte) in Pinar del Río, Cuba, where I had very strict and magnificent teachers (Gilberto, Tomás Torre, Néstor Luis and Héctor). Among others, I would like to thank my professors of solfeggio, music history and piano.

To my great friends and fellow students of my graduating class (Omar Rojas, Ciro Parlá, Eddie Pérez, Jorge Castillo, Iván González, Iliana Castillo, Ademilis Hernández) who gave me advice and were companions in my life.

I'd also like to acknowledge the presence of a person whom I greatly respect and admire: José Luis Quintana (Changuito) for teaching me the beauty, technique and magic of the Conga. Along with me, other students like Yoel del Sol, Carlos Reyes, Pedro Pablo Martínez had the opportunity to learn this marvelous style.

I would like to mention another special person in my life, Adolfo Orta, my trombone teacher, who was not just my teacher but my friend as well. I want to express my gratitude to my teacher of Batá, Nardo (el Goyo) who gave me the opportunity to learn an instrument so beautiful and rich in rhythm, who helped me and allowed me to combine the rhythms of Batá with the Conga.

It's very important to acknowledge the musicians with whom I played and recorded: Yoel Páez, Yoel Domínguez, Sergio Noroña, Frank Rubio, Yosvel Bernal, Alexander Abreu, Joaquín Díaz, Carlos Pérez, Juan Manuel Ceruto, for helping me enrich my mind with their knowledge.

I would like to talk about the most important person in the process of creating this book, a person of great intelligence, whom I thank for creating the idea to make this book: Kevin Moore. Also, to thank Mike Gerald for having dedicated some of his time to write with great speed this method of percussion and Orlando Fiol for having given us the benefit of his great experience in the creation of these books.

In this acknowledgment, I'd also like to mention the conga players who were my models to follow: Jorge Alfonso (El Niño) and Angá (Irakere), Andrés Miranda (Negrón), Tomás Ramos, Juan Nogueras (Wickly), Tata Güines, los Papines, el Goyo (teacher at I.S.A.), José Luis Quintana (Changuito), Manolo (Los Van Van), El Yulo (NG La Banda), Yoel Drigs, etc.

I would also like to express my gratitude to timba.com, Duniel Deya, and to my friends in California who helped me during my stay over there: Michel, Johann, Alexey Berlind, Alain, Fito, Bárbara Valladares, Javier, Osvaldo, and Joanna Goldberg.

I hope that this new and different method will help all conga players develop their Timba technique in a fast and efficient way, so that the world will soon see more good conga players.

Kevin Moore, Mike Gerald & Orlando Fiol wish to thank:

Conceptual Guidance: David Peñalosa, Alexey Berlind, and Pepe Martínez.
Production: Neal Hellman, Sarah Belden, Jon Hansen, Doug Witherspoon, Ed Riegler, Christy Meyer, Bill Bay, Trevor Salloum, and above all, our graphics gurus, Bill Wolfer and Mig Gianino.
Photography: Tom Ehrlich (additional photos by Kevin Moore, Duniel Deya and Yoel Páez)
Moral and Technical Support: Wendy Black, Kathryn Van Eenoo, Tanja Cruz, Edduar Bernal, Jorge Ginorio, Juan Tomás García, Javier Muñiz, Mike Lazarus, José Reyes, Mike Doran, María Carlota Domandi, Luis Carranza, Joanna Goldberg, Bosco Gitano, Elena Peña & Nikki, Bruce Ishikawa, Majela Serrano, Hugo Cancio, Arnaldo Vargas, Nina "La Reina del Merengue" Gómez, Curtis Lanoue.
Inspiration: Rebeca Mauleón-Santana, Alberto Centelles, Juan Ceruto, Yosvel Bernal, Yoel Páez, Yoel Domínguez, Giraldo Piloto, Calixto Oviedo, Reinier Guerra, Yulién Oviedo, Michael Spiro, Andrés Cuayo, Sergio Noroña, Carlos Caro, and above all, Tomás Cruz for his patience, perseverance and incredible insights into the secrets of music.

PART 1: INTRODUCTION

The Tomás Cruz Conga Method

What?

The Tomás Cruz Conga Method is designed to quickly and comprehensively teach anyone, from a rank beginner to a professional conguero, to play congas as they're played in Cuba today. It can be studied using only the book, only the DVD (Digital Video Disc), or a combination of the two. This book, Volume III, is the most advanced and assumes that the reader already has the ability to play basic congas in a Latin music context.

Who?

Tomás "Tomasito" Cruz was born and raised in Cuba in the middle of the musical revolution of the 90's. By the time he relocated to Miami he had become one of the top congueros in Cuba, playing in what most Cuban music experts consider one of the two or three best Timba bands ever assembled, the 1997-98 incarnation of Paulito FG y su Élite which recorded the groundbreaking CD, "Con la conciencia tranquila". The creativity and drive of Tomasito's conga tumbaos on that album put him in the very upper echelon of the most competitive Latin music scene in the world. Similarly, it took Tomasito very little time to rise to the top of the Miami Latin music scene, playing with Manolín, el Médico de la Salsa, Willie Chirino, Celia Cruz, and many others. He also has a thorough mastery of bongó, Batá, and a deep understanding of Cuban music as a whole. In short, when we set out to write a book explaining the mysteries of Cuban conga playing, Tomasito was our first choice by a considerable margin.

Why?

For many years it was extremely difficult to find recordings of modern Cuban music, much less to hear the bands live, but in the late 90's groups like Los Van Van and Paulito FG y su Élite began to tour the US, Europe and Japan, and Latin music fans and musicians alike were amazed when they heard the exciting new "Timba" style they were playing. However, many of those who tried to learn this new approach found it significantly more difficult to understand than the Salsa commonly played outside of Cuba. Every instrument of the rhythm section had taken a quantum leap in terms of complexity and creative freedom.

This book was written in response to the three most common problems we've encountered among those trying to tackle modern Cuban conga drumming.

Problem #1: What exactly are they playing? Even those who have taken study courses in Cuba, which invariably seem limited to the fundamentals and history of traditional Cuban music, have found themselves just as dumbfounded upon hearing the modern groups in performance. In addition to the language and cultural barriers, the music is too new for the players themselves to have fully analyzed it...they're too busy *playing* it and adding to it to take time to dissect it and explain it. The albums themselves have so much going on that even professional musicians have difficulty transcribing individual parts by ear and the Timba style is so ambidextrous that even knowing whether to slap with the left or right hand becomes part of the jigsaw puzzle.

Solution: All of the patterns in Volume III are from real Timba albums, clearly notated, and spoon-fed stroke by stroke to the reader by means of a simple DVD method.

Problem #2: Where did it come from? How did they get from Salsa to this? The musicians cite the influences of *Songo, Batá* music, *Rumba, Guaguancó,* and even American funk and R&B, but how are these influences actually incorporated into the actual rhythm section parts?

Solution: Volume II uses the same innovative video teaching technique to teach a well-organized and clearly explained compendium of the rhythms that form the roots of Timba.

Problem #3: How do they play like that? These young musicians play with such fire and grace that trying to emulate them can be discouraging. How, without having been born and raised in Havana, can musicians get a little piece of that magic into their own playing?

Solution: Volume I spells out the method used to teach congas in the Cuban conservatories and the hours of DVD footage included in this course provide the opportunity to learn the feel of Cuban drumming by osmosis; to watch and play along with a master conguero as he breaks each pattern down stroke by stroke, with a steady rhythm groove playing throughout the exercise.

How?

At the heart of the Tomás Cruz Conga Method is a simple and effective DVD technique based on learning by imitation. Once you understand the simple process explained below, it's actually quite possible to learn each pattern with only the DVD, without reading music at all.

Tomasito plays the pattern at full speed, and then, in slow motion, accompanied by a special click track, he plays only the first stroke of the pattern and then waits for the beginning of the pattern to come around again. He repeats just the first stroke a total of 4 times. This gives the student 4 chances to learn and practice the hand movement, allowing Tomasito's tone, posture, time feel and technique to be assimilated "by osmosis", as he himself assimilated it by watching the greatest congueros of earlier generations during his childhood and adolescence in Cuba.

Tomás then adds the second stroke and repeats *this* cycle 4 times; then the third, and so on until the pattern is complete. It's extremely easy to keep up with the flow of the DVD because only a single stroke is added every four repetitions, and since each DVD chapter can be started over without the tedious rewinding necessary with a video tape, it's easy to go back to the beginning if you lose your place in the pattern. Thanks to the huge capacity of DVD discs, we were able to film Tomasito patiently building many of the patterns in this way. From the very beginning the student is playing in rhythm, and in clave, asked to learn only a single stroke at a time, and given the chance to master it before each additional stroke is added. Patterns that are too long to be appropriate for this method are demonstrated at full speed and in slow motion.

About the Coauthors

Kevin Moore is the music editor of the world's largest Cuban music website, www.timba.com, and the musical director of the American salsa band Orquesta Gitano (www.picadillo.com/gitano). He has studied with dozens of leading Cuban musicians, written many extensive articles on Cuban music, and served as a consultant for features and articles produced by the BBC, the Los Angeles Times, and musicologists from Harvard and other major universities.

Michael Gerald is a Canadian drummer who has spent 7 years studying and playing Timba and has recorded two albums with his group, Sol y Soul (solysoul.timba.com), which, aside from himself, is composed entirely of all-stars from the various Cuban supergroups.

Orlando Fiol, a professional pianist/conguero/composer in the Philadelphia area, began his studies of Latin music as a small child under the tutelage of his father, Latin recording artist Henry Fiol. In 1996 he traveled to Cuba where he studied and played with Pancho Quinto, Changuito, members of Sierra Maestra, Raíces Profundas and the Sexteto Habanero. He is also an expert in the fields of Jazz, classical music and Indian music, having been awarded a fellowship to study tabla and pakhawaj in India. Orlando's encyclopedic knowledge of the history of folkloric and Latin music, and his ability to communicate with Tomasito in fluent Spanish have proved indispensable in the writing of this series.

What is Timba?

Timba is the commonly accepted term for the new type of concert and dance music that's been played in Cuba since about 1989. For about half of that time it was impossible to hear live Timba without going to Cuba, and nearly as hard to acquire Timba recordings. To further complicate matters, music produced in Cuba was and still is, to a great degree, "blacklisted" in the United States and nearly never played on commercial radio. In spite of all these obstacles, Timba groups have been touring the United States and Europe regularly for the last 6 years and have inspired a rapidly growing, almost fanatic following, including American musicians such as coauthors Kevin Moore, Michael Gerald and Orlando Fiol.

The musical genre most closely related to Timba is Salsa, but Timba also contains strong influences from Afro-Cuban folkloric music, American R&B, Jazz, and various other forms of world pop music. A huge emphasis is placed on originality — not only in songwriting and arranging, but in the individual patterns played by each member of the rhythm section, and while this has resulted in a large number of classic recordings, it's also led to a great deal of frustration among musicians trying to learn to play Timba because the rhythm patterns are sometimes unique to each song. Helping people understand this wide range of rhythmic diversity is the primary goal of this series of books.

Who are the Leading Timba Bands?

There are about a dozen major Timba groups, with new ones springing up from time to time, and frequent shifting of key players from one band to another. The musical scene in Havana is so strong and closely-knit that each band seems to feed off the creativity of the others.

The most important groups, in approximate order of their appearance on the Timba scene, are Los Van Van, NG La Banda, Charanga Habanera, Issac Delgado, Paulito FG, El Médico de la Salsa, Klimax, Bamboleo, Manolito y su Trabuco, Azúcar Negra, Los Que Son Son and Tirso Duarte.

Tomás Cruz played with Paulito FG and currently plays with El Médico de la Salsa (also known as Manolín). He played congas on four of the most important albums of the Timba genre:

Paulito FG: "Con la conciencia tranquila" (Nueva Fania NF-108)
Juan Ceruto: "Gracias Formell" (Ciocan Records HMC-2607)
Paulito FG: "El bueno soy yo" (also released as "Paulito FG") (Nueva Fania NF-104)
Manolín, El Médico de la Salsa: "El puente" (Ciocan Records HMC-2605)

To learn more about Timba we recommend the website www.timba.com, which contains well over 100,000 words of articles and interviews edited by coauthor Kevin Moore (kevin@timba.com). There are also extensive audio examples and educational materials.

Who are the other leading Timba congueros?

There are literally hundreds of phenomenal congueros in Cuba. Here's an incomplete list of some of the leading Timba congueros who tour outside of Cuba frequently. Each has his own page on www.timba.com, as does Tomasito (http://tomasito.timba.com).

Denis "Papacho" Savón
Issac Delgado Group
http://papacho.timba.com

Jorge Luis "Papiosco" Torres
founding member of Klimax
now tours with Cubanismo
http://papiosco.timba.com

Tomás "El Panga" Ramos
Tomasito's predecessor in
Paulito FG y su Élite
http://panga.timba.com

Duñesky Barreto
Bamboleo
http://dunesky.timba.com

Alexis "Mipa" Cuesta
Tomasito's predecessor with
El Médico de la Salsa
http://mipa.timba.com

Orlando Mengual
Charanga Habanera
http://orlandito.timba.com

Jorge "El Toro" Castillo
Los Que Son Son
http://eltoro.timba.com

Evelio Ramos
Manolito y su Trabuco
http://evelio.timba.com

Manuel "Manolo" Labarrera
Los Van Van
http://manolo.timba.com

Luis Guillermo Palacio
Carlos Manuel y su Clan; Sol y Soul

Yoel Cuesta
Azúcar Negra
(now with Adalberto Alvarez)
http://yoelcuesta.timba.com

Adel González
Irakere

Wickly Nogueras
original conguero of NG La Banda
http://wickly.timba.com

PART II: CLAVE

What is Clave?

Entire books have been devoted to this question! In this book the term "clave" refers to the endlessly fascinating 5-stroke rhythm upon which virtually all Latin music is based. An essential part of learning to play congas, or any instrument in a Latin context, is to "internalize" the clave, and for this reason, every exercise in this series is designed to be practiced while listening to the clave rhythm. The accompanying DVD uses a clave click track at all times.

Volumes I & II each contain an extensive Appendix discussing Clave in great detail.

There are three different clave rhythms used in this series, and each can be thought of as starting from the beginning or from the halfway point. *See p. 15 for a discussion on the use of 16th notes versus 8th notes. The appendix contains each example rewritten in 8ths for those who prefer that method of notation.*

Rumba Clave is the primary clave of Timba and is used slightly more often in its 2-3 form.

DVD Chapter 1: 3-2 Rumba Clave

DVD Chapter 2: 2-3 Rumba Clave

Note that the two patterns are identical except for their starting points. The phrasing of the melodic and harmonic instruments determine whether the listener perceives the clave rhythm as beginning on the "2-side" or the "3-side".

In the DVD Chapters, Tomás gives a countoff and plays an appropriate conga part while singing each clave rhythm. Note that regardless of the clave, Tomasito always starts his conga pattern on the 2-side. We'll discuss this further later in the book.

Son Clave, which Tomasito calls *clave cubana,* is the primary clave of Salsa, but is also sometimes used in Timba, especially during the opening section, or *cuerpo,* of the arrangement. As you can see, Rumba and Son Clave differ only by the placement of one stroke. Some groups, such as Charanga Habanera, use *only* Rumba Clave while others, such as Los Van Van and Issac Delgado, substitute one for the other freely.

For the first 5 DVD chapters we asked Tomasito to sing the clave patterns and accompany himself on congas, intentionally avoiding any discussion as to what type of conga accompaniment to use. The results are extremely interesting! Note that in the 3-2 examples, he sings the clave on the 3-side but starts playing the congas on the pickup to the 2-side. Keep this in mind as you continue on your journey towards understanding Cuban rhythms!

DVD Chapter 3: 3-2 Son Clave

DVD Chapter 4: 2-3 Son Clave

6/8 Clave is almost never the *primary* clave in Timba or Salsa, but a key feature of the Timba groove is the presence of 6/8 cross-rhythms rooted in Afro-Cuban folkloric music. Tomasito, who is intimately familar with both sacred and secular folkoric music, is particularly fond of using 6/8 rhythms during the Pedal sections which will be covered in great detail later in this book. Examples of conga patterns which use 6/8 clave as the primary clave can be found in Volume II.

DVD Chapter 5: 6/8 Clave

Although written in 6/8, it usually makes more sense to think of these rhythms in triplets as evidenced by the way Tomasito counts in DVD Chapter 5. From a Jazz, Funk, or R&B perspective, the use of 6/8 rhythms in Timba could be compared to implying a shuffle feel against a straight 16th note groove. But to truly grasp this subtle but critical aspect of modern Cuban music, it's necessary to become familiar with the Batá and Rumba rhythms that form the common cultural foundation of the Cuban musicians who invented Timba. Fortunately, in contrast to Timba, there's a wealth of educational material on Cuban folkloric music, such as those recommended on the following page.

Recommended Books on Afro-Cuban Folkloric Music:
"Rumba Guaguancó Conversations", by Arturo Rodríguez, also published by Mel Bay
"The Music of Santería", by John Amira, published by White Cliffs Media
"Sectional Transcriptions of the Orú Igbodú" by Gary Greenberg

Recommended Recordings of Afro-Cuban Folkloric Music:
-Sacred Music: "Grupo Ilu Aña - Sacred Rhythms" (Bembe 2027)
-Secular Music: "Los Muñequitos de Matanzas" (any recordings, especially those from the 1950's)

Recommended Internet Articles on Clave:
-"Clave and Clave Changes in the music of Charanga Habanera"
-"The Four Great Clave Debates"
Both can be found at www.timba.com. A shortcut internet address for these articles is: http://clave.timba.com

Special Note: "The big drum on the 3-side" concept

A commonly taught concept in Salsa conga-playing is the idea that the conguero "marks" the clave by playing two open strokes on the low drum on the 3-side of the clave, like this:

B T S T B T O O N T S O O T O O
L L R L L L R R L L R R R L R R

Many top salsa congueros consider it wrong (in some cases *very wrong)* to play the above tumba figure on the 2-side of the clave. This is absolutely not the case in Timba! There are many instances in Timba where the above pattern is played just as written, in 2-3 clave, but just as many where two identically placed open tumba tones are played on the 2-side. For example, check out Tomasito's use of the big drum in DVD Chapters 1-4 as he demonstrates the clave.

The "big drum on the 3-side" concept is one of several sacrosanct laws of Salsa which must be taken with a grain of salt if one is to fully grasp Timba. Another such "law" which is routinely broken by Timba arrangers is the idea that an arrangement never be constructed such that the same side of the clave is played twice in a row. See clave.timba.com and the Clave appendices of Volumes I & II for more on this one.

PART 3: LEARNING TIMBA MARCHAS

What's a Marcha?

A *marcha,* sometimes called a *tumbao,* is a rhythm pattern used by the conguero or drummer to keep time. A marcha can last one, two, or even four claves before repeating itself, and may include improvisations to respond musically to other elements of the arrangement. The different sections of a Timba arrangement will usually have different marchas.

In Salsa, and most other types of Latin music, conga marchas are fairly standardized, but in Timba there's a huge amount of variation and creativity. In some cases the conguero will even invent a completely new marcha to fit a specific arrangement.

How are the Marchas Notated?

First of all, remember that it's quite possible to learn many of these patterns without ever looking at the notation. Our Step by Step DVD training Method allows you to learn them interactively by watching Tomasito and copying his hand movements. We've also tried to devise the clearest possible method of notation, which includes specially shaped noteheads and two lines of letters beneath the notes. The upper line designates the type of stroke and the lower lines shows whether it's played with the left or right hand.

For example:

Thus, even if you don't read music, and/or haven't learned the note shapes, you can learn the pattern by looking at the letters. The first row starts out with S B T S, which stands for Slap, Bass, Tip, Slap. The second row starts out with R L L R, which stands for Right, Left, Left, Right. When, as in the case of the 11th note, both hands play at the same time, one hand is written above and the other below. Alternatively, we sometimes write "S/O" instead of placing the second note above. See Volume I for a full course on each of these strokes.

Some of Tomasito's recordings use two congas and others use three. The high drum is written on the top space ("E"), the middle drum on the middle line ("B"), and the low drum on the bottom space ("F").

Open tones are notated with a round, solid notehead. The *tumba* (or *hembra* or "big drum") and *tres dos* (middle) drums are almost always played open. Note that we use the term *"quinto"* to refer to the smallest of the drums used in popular music, not to be confused with the even smaller and higher pitched *"quinto"* drum used exclusively in Rumba music.

quinto | tres dos | tumba

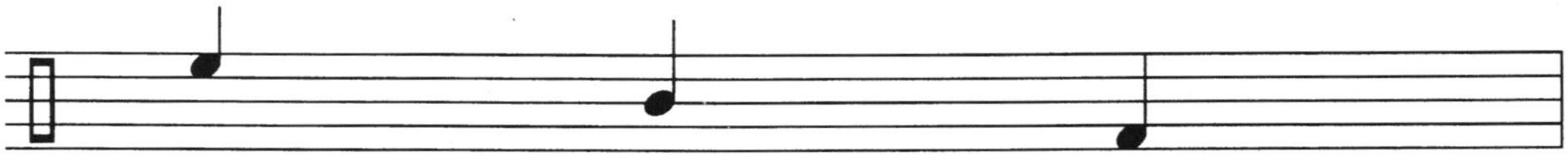

high drum | middle drum | low drum

The *quinto* (or *macho* or high drum) also uses up to seven other strokes, which are described and demonstrated in great detail in Volume 1:

Spanish =>	abierto	tapado	semi–tapado	bajo

English =>	open	slap	open slap	bass
As notated =>	O	S	OS	B

Spanish =>	punta	falso	bajo falso	presionado

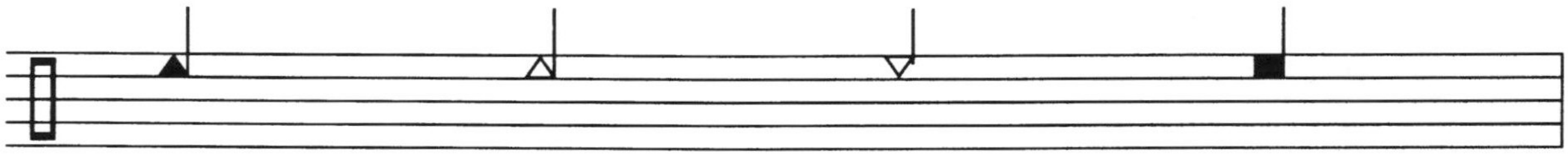

English =>	tip	ghost	bass ghost	muff
As notated =>	T	G	BG	M

16^{ths} versus 8^{ths}

There's a lot of controversy over whether Cuban rhythms should be written in 8th or 16th notes. Writing in 16th notes is more common in Cuba while most American and European groups write their music in 8th notes. Each method has its advantages.

In terms of describing what's really taking place in the music there's no doubt that the 16th note approach is superior. All professional Latin musicians, regardless of how they notate it, *feel* the music such that there are only 4 beats per clave but writing it in 8th notes implies that there are eight. Trying to hear the beat twice as fast as it really is causes severe conceptual problems for students. Experienced musicians learn to look at 8th notes and play them in "cut time" so that they're feeling the beat correctly, but taking advantage of the fact that the 8th note notation is less cluttered with extra flags and beams and therefore easier on the eyes.

We have no desire to confuse students *or* to inconvenience experienced musicians who are already used to reading in 8^{ths}, so in each volume we provide appendices with all of the patterns written in 8^{ths} (see Part 9, beginning at page 64). For more on this subject, please see the "Clave" appendices of Volumes I & II.

How to Use the Step-by-Step DVD Training Method

At the heart of the Tomás Cruz Conga Method is a simple and effective new method of learning marchas by playing along with the enclosed DVD video. Here's how it works:

Let's look at the first marcha from Part 3, for example:

There are 2 DVD chapters for each marcha, in this case, chapters 6 & 7.

In DVD Chapter 6, Tomasito plays the marcha at full speed. Listen to this a few times until the marcha pattern becomes familiar. If you have the recording, listen to the title track of "Con la conciencia tranquila" to hear the marcha in a musical context. It occurs right at the beginning of the song and returns when the band goes into Bomba gear (explained later) at the 2:47 mark.

Singing along with the full speed DVD chapter is also an excellent idea. Make sure you hear and understand where the clave click track is before proceeding! If there's any doubt in your mind, review DVD Chapter 2, which demonstrates the 2-3 rumba clave used for this marcha.

Now go to DVD Chapter 7. This time the tempo is much slower. Listen carefully to the clave click track and clap along to again make sure you're hearing the clave correctly. Some very famous Timba arrangers have confided to us that they *intentionally* invent ambiguous rhythms which can trick the listener into thinking the downbeat is somewhere other than where it really is! Once you've gotten a rhythm stuck in your head with the wrong orientation it takes four times as long to relearn it the right way! So take our word for it: *always, always, ALWAYS, know where the clave is before you start learning a rhythm!*

Once the clave feels right, you're ready to start the exercise. Set up your congas so you can sit comfortably in front of your television set. Tomasito plays just the first stroke of the pattern, waits for the clave to run its course, and then repeats this cycle for a total of four times. As you watch the DVD, play along. It will be very easy because only one stroke is added at a time and you're given four chances to practice it before the next one is added. To warn you in advance what the next stroke will be there's also a vocal cue exactly 2 beats, or half a clave, before the beginning of the measure that contains the new stroke.

Every 4 claves, another stroke is added. You may not make it all the way through the exercise the first time, but thanks to the miracle of DVD, you need only press a button to return to the beginning, or to review Chapter 6 to get the sound of the full speed marcha back into your ear. At the first sign of frustration, just start over. *Don't worry about how long it takes* – just keep your level of frustration completely under control by starting over whenever necessary.

Learning complex marchas doesn't have to be hard if you only add one new stroke at a time. The whole idea of this exercise is that it's supposed to be easy. As soon as you feel yourself "trying", grab that remote control and start the exercise over. Remember that what you're learning subconsciously from staring at Tomasito's hands is *more* important than learning the pattern itself – it's the nuances of rhythm, tone and feeling that make his recordings and performances so satisfying and by practicing along with the DVD each day you'll begin to absorb these qualities into your own playing. The feeling of "swing" is difficult or impossible to explain in words, and there's no doubt that the best, if not the *only* way to learn it is the way Tomás himself learned it...by "osmosis". In Cuba, these subtleties are handed down from generation to generation by example – not by explanation – and you can use the DVD to let Tomasito hand a little of his magic down to you.

Play along with DVD Chapter 7 every day until you can play the full pattern effortlessly enough to start practicing with the full speed version, DVD Chapter 6.

Where Does the Exercise Start and Why?

This is perhaps the most confusing aspect of learning Cuban rhythms. About half of the melodies and chord progressions in Cuban music start on the 3-side and the other half on the 2-side. When someone says "*Llamada anónima* is in 3-2", it simply means that the musical phrases of that particular song begin on the 3-side of the rhythm pattern played by the percussionists. But Cuban percussionists, while fully cognizant of this, still conceive of all of *their* patterns as beginning on the 2-side. Take a look at DVD Chapters 1-4, in which Tomasito sings each clave pattern while accompanying himself on congas. In Chapters 2 & 4, which are in 2-3 clave, he begins the conga marcha immediately, but in Chapters 1 & 3, which are in 3-2 clave, he starts singing first and then begins the conga marcha on the pickup to the 2-side.

One theory to explain this is that the 2-side accentuates the downbeat and 3-side accentuates the upbeats and thus, most fills tend to fall on the 3-side and most patterns feel more natural starting on the 2-side.

Our solution to this admittedly confusing musical phenomenon is to begin the exercise where Tomasito hears it beginning, but to notate it so that the downbeats and repeat signs correspond to the musical phrases of the song in which the marcha was recorded.

A black downward triangle and a text note clearly indicate the starting point of each Step by Step DVD exercise.

PART 4:
MARCHAS WITH STEP BY STEP DVD TRAINING

Marchas from Tomasito's Recordings with Paulito FG

Marcha #1 - DVD Chapters 6 & 7

Clave: 2-3 Rumba
Tempo: 92
Album: Paulito FG: Con la conciencia tranquila
Song: *Con la conciencia tranquila,* 0:00 & 2:47

NOTES: Tomasito calls this a *Marcha Bomba.* This could mean that it contains elements of the Puerto Rican Bomba Sicá rhythm, or that it's appropriate to use when the band is in the Bomba "gear", a rhythm section mode unique to Timba. Both meanings apply here.

1) The traditional Puerto Rican Bomba rhythm: This rhythm, covered in Volume II , has been influential in the development of Timba. Sometimes the rhythm will be used in its entirety for certain sections of an arrangement (see Marcha #8 and the arrangement analysis in Part 7), but references to the Bomba rhythm also find their way into normal Timba marchas, as is the case here. The last three open tones of Marcha #1, (shown above with a bracket), create the Bomba flavor, while the rest of the marcha is Timba, especially the *doble tapado* figure at the beginning.

2) The Bomba section: The Bomba section is a special rhythm section mode, or "gear", which is very common in Timba and covered in detail in Part 6 of this book. The most obvious feature of the Bomba section as used by most Timba groups, including Paulito FG and Manolín, is that the bassist stops his marcha and slides the right hand down the low string of the bass, emulating the low drum parts in various types of folkloric music. The conga marchas used in Bomba sections vary quite a bit and may or may not include references to the Puerto Rican Bomba rhythm. This particular marcha is used in a Bomba section at 2:47 of *Con la conciencia tranquila.*

Finally, as explained in Part 2, don't be confused by the two open tumba tones on the 2-side. Although traditional salsa often reserves this figure to mark the 3-side, this is not always the case in Timba and this marcha is most definitely in 2-3 clave.

Marcha #2 - DVD Chapters 8 & 9

Clave: 3-2 Rumba
Tempo: 92
Album: Paulito FG: Con la conciencia tranquila
Song: *¿Y ahora qué?*, 3:12 (coro 2)

NOTES: Tomasito calls this a *Marcha Cumbia* because the open tones recall the Colombian Cumbia marchas covered in Volume II. The other elements are chosen to relate to a specific Timba arrangement, Paulito FG's *¿Y ahora qué?* For example, the four repeated muff tones reinforce the now legendary piano tumbao that Sergio Noroña plays during the second coro section.

¿Y ahora qué? is one of the most strange and beautiful creations in all of Timba. Pay special attention to the cuartal harmonies and unusual cadences in the piano and bass tumbaos as well as the phrasing of the vocals in this section.

Note that although *Y ahora qué* starts in 2-3, the clave changes to 3-2 when this marcha enters. There are several ways that Timba "changes clave" (see http://clave.timba.com for more on this). This song does so "by the book", by changing the time signature of the measure which starts at 3:00 from 4/4 to 2/4. Thus, without interrupting the continuous flow of the clave, the harmonic phrases after this point begin on the 3-side. So the section in which this marcha is used is in 3-2 clave. As explained earlier, Tomasito begins all exercises on the 2-side of the clave, as shown by the "DVD exercise starts here" marking.

Marcha #3 - DVD Chapters 10 & 11

Clave: 3-2 Rumba
Tempo: 92
Album: Paulito FG: Con la conciencia tranquila
Song: *¿Y ahora qué?*, 4:25 (coro 3), also *No te lo creas*, 4:26 (mambo 2)

NOTES: This marcha, whose rhythms are derived from folkloric music, is used almost exclusively when the band is playing in the Bomba gear (see Part 6 of this book for a full description of "gears"). Unlike Marcha #1, this one is not related to the Puerto Rican Bomba.

In *¿Y ahora qué?* it's used in 3-2 and the two open tumba tones come in the middle of the measure. In *No te lo creas,* a different song from the same album, (and the arrangement which is analyzed in its entirety in Part 7), the same marcha appears in 2-3, also in a Bomba section, with the second tumba tone coming as the downbeat of the measure.

In the music of Paulito FG, Manolín, and some other Timba groups, these are the most important notes of the bass part as well, and an extremely reliable indicator of where the 2-side is. Whenever the bassist slides his hand down the low string on a downbeat, that's the downbeat of the 2-side. In contrast, the earlier group NG la Banda placed the bass slide on the upbeats of 2 & 4. One of the most exciting aspects of Timba is that Bomba and other rhythm section "gears" continue to evolve and change.

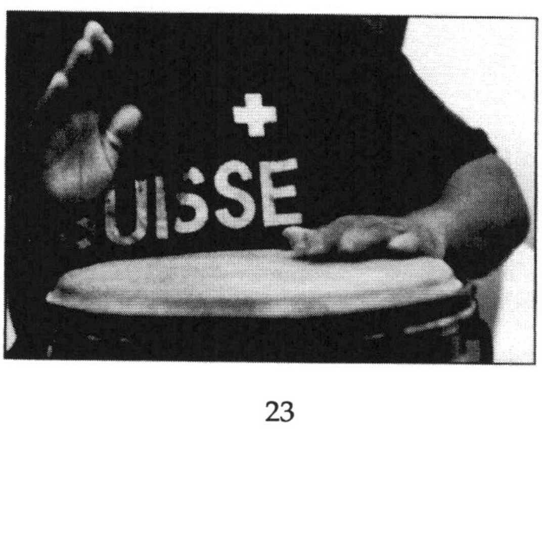

Marcha #4 - DVD Chapters 12 & 13

Clave: 2-3 Rumba
Tempo: 93.5
Album: Paulito FG: Con la conciencia tranquila
Song: *Entre dos amigos*, 3:56, mambo 2 w/rhythm section in bomba gear

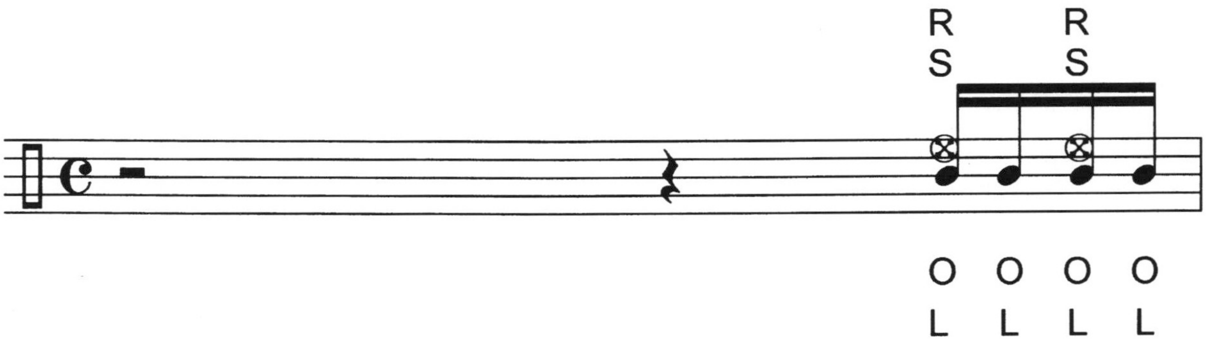

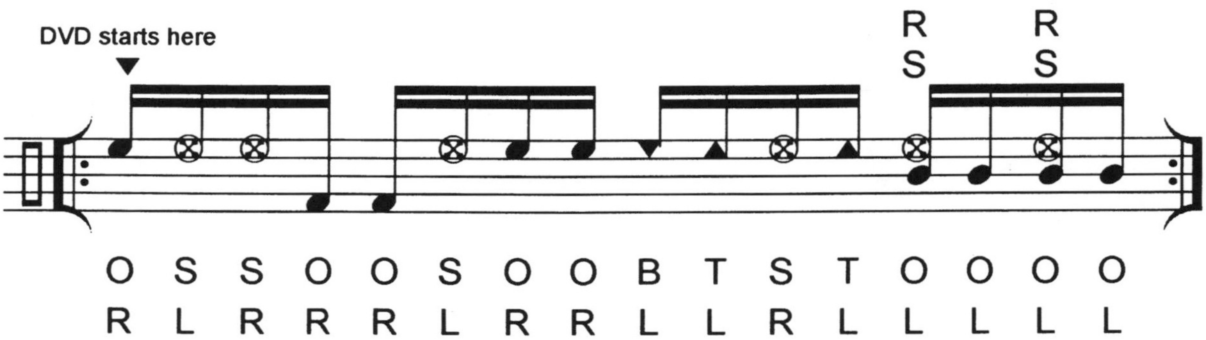

NOTES: This marcha comes in during a section which demonstrates many of the key differences between Timba and traditional Salsa. While the lead vocalist continues to improvise, a new coro *and* a new horn mambo are introduced simultaneously. In Salsa, each of these three elements of the arrangement would have a separate section. To top it off, at this same point, the rhythm section goes into the Bomba gear (explained in detail in Part 6).

Another interesting feature of this marcha is the interesting effect created by slapping the quinto while playing the middle drum open.

Also note the common Timba figure of the double slap *(doble tapado)* on the middle two 16th notes of the first beat.

Marcha #5 - DVD Chapters 14 & 15

Clave: 3-2 Rumba
Tempo: 105
Album: Paulito FG: Con la conciencia tranquila
Song: *Llamada anónima,* 0:00, introduction

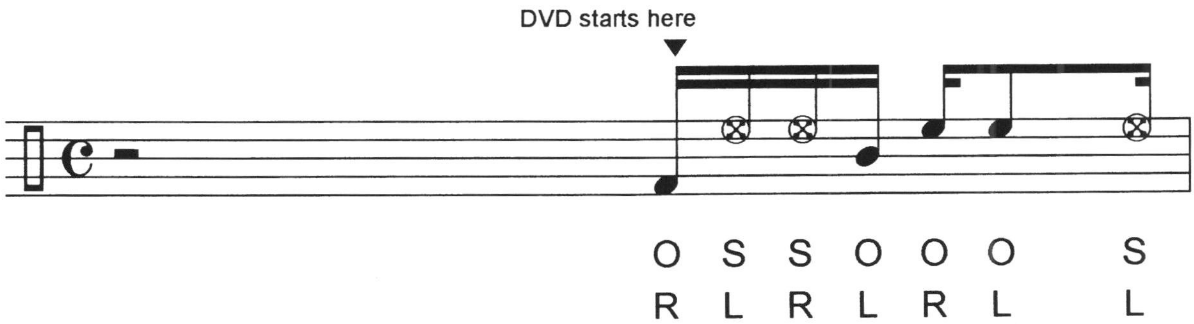

*** BG=Bass Ghost**

NOTES: Tomasito calls this a *Marcha Makuta*. Makuta is a dance rhythm of Congolese origin used in Palo ceremonies in Afro-Cuban folkloric music. Tomás is currently working on a fourth book which will be devoted entirely to folkloric rhythms including, among others, Guaguancó, Makuta, and Batá music.

The marcha is very distinctive and very far removed from the traditional conga tumbao. Note the complete absence of the most common rhythmic unit of Latin conga playing, the "bass-tip-slap" figure. In its normal place at the beginning of the measure is the double slap found in Marchas 1, 2, & 4, but now it's placed so that the second slap falls on the downbeat. Another double slap occurs on beat 3, this time in the middle of the beat as it did in the previous marchas.

This is an example of a marcha custom-designed to fit an arrangement, *Llamada anónima,* one of Paulito FG's most popular hits. *Llamada anónima* has a relentless groove, and at 105 BPM is quite a bit faster than normal Timba and Salsa. The bass and drums have more of a pop feel than most Timba and are nicely balanced by the folkloric elements of the conga part.

This marcha makes an excellent exercise for getting comfortable playing melodically on all three drums.

Marcha #6 - DVD Chapters 16 & 17

Clave: 3-2 Rumba
Tempo: 105
Album: Paulito FG: Con la conciencia tranquila
Song: *Llamada anónima,* 0:34, cuerpo: section A

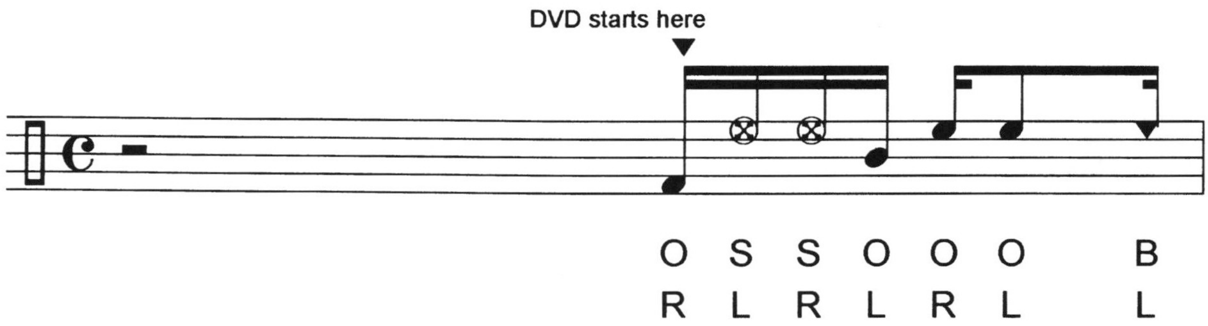

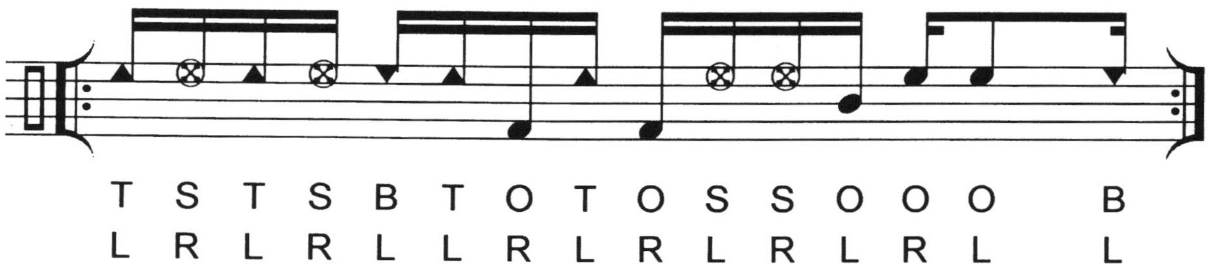

NOTES: This is a variation of the previous marcha, designed to fit the cuerpo of the song. Here, the "bass-tip-slap" returns, but note that it's rhythmically displaced to start on the pickup rather than the downbeat. Tomás frequently creates new rhythms by taking common hand patterns and placing them in unusual parts of the measure.

Marcha #7 - DVD Chapters 18 & 19

Clave: 3-2 Rumba
Tempo: 105
Album: Paulito FG: Con la conciencia tranquila
Song: *Llamada anónima,* 4:32

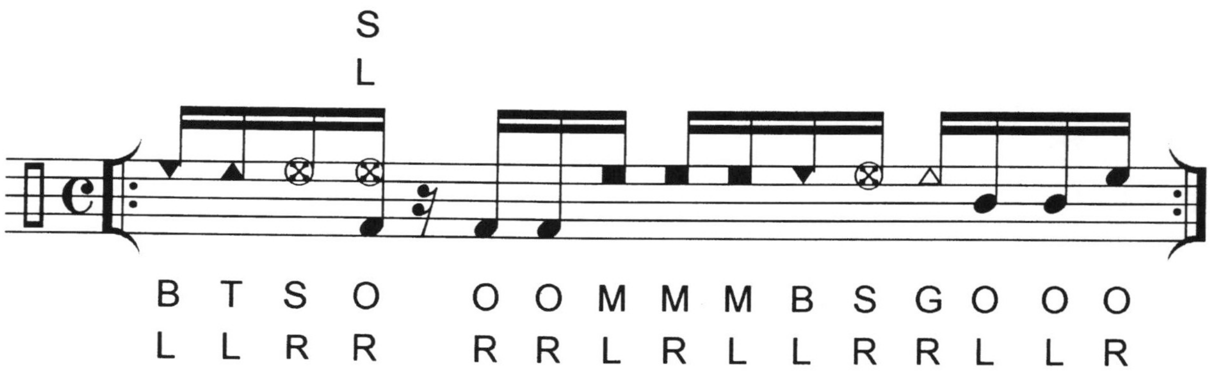

NOTES: This marcha, also from *Llamada anónima,* provides a change of pace from the Makuta rhythm. It comes in near the end of the arrangement during Mambo 3, when the band goes from Bomba back to a regular marcha gear. Like Marcha #4, it combines a slap with an open tone, (this time the tumba), and the double slap is displaced to yet another part of the beat.

Marcha #8 - DVD Chapters 20 & 21

Clave: 2-3 Rumba
Tempo: 94
Album: Paulito FG: Con la conciencia tranquila
Song: *No te lo creas*, 0:00, 0:52, 1:38

NOTES: This marcha and the next two are particularly important, as they're from *No te lo creas*, the arrangement we chose for the complete analysis in Part 7. This opening rhythm, which comes back two more times during the cuerpo, is very close to the real Puerto Rican Bomba Sicá, as opposed to the hybrid Timba Bomba gear used later in the arrangement.

Since the Bomba rhythm is not really in clave, you'll notice that the DVD's click track replaces the usual clave with a Bomba figure. The "clave-neutral" nature of this groove comes in handy in the overall arrangement as it allows a smooth transition from 3-2 to 2-3 without having to insert a bar of 2/4.

Another interesting feature of this marcha is the contrapuntal effect created by the slaps and opens. The slaps play a steady accompaniment figure of dotted 8ths and 16ths, played alternately "left-right" and "right-left", while the open tones add the Puerto Rican Bomba flavor.

Tomasito with Manolín in Miami
Photo by Duniel Deya

Marcha #9 - DVD Chapters 22 & 23

Clave: 3-2 Rumba
Tempo: 94
Album: Paulito FG: Con la conciencia tranquila
Song: *No te lo creas,* 0:32, 1:18

O G O S S O O O
R L R R L R R L

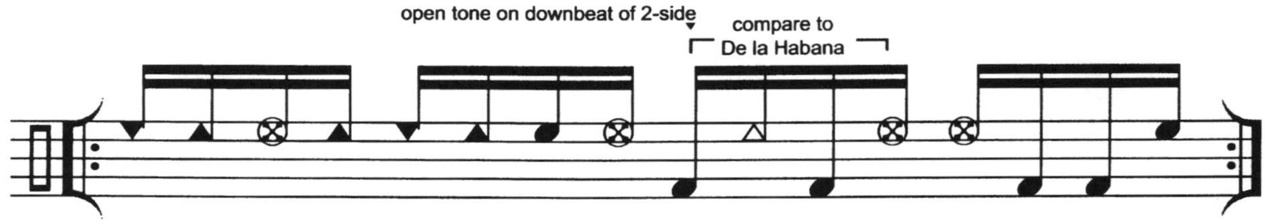

B T S T B T O S O G O S S O O O
L L R L L L R L R L R R L R R L

NOTES: Some of Tomasito's most interesting original marchas feature the open tumba drum on the downbeat of the 2-side of the clave, usually when the section in question is in 3-2 clave. This particular one is used for the cuerpo of *No te lo creas,* but only on the B section, where the tumba tones fall very nicely between the phrases of the lead vocal. As we'll see in the full analysis of *No te lo creas* in Part 7, Tomasito uses a different marcha for each of the three sections of that cuerpo.

After you master this marcha, compare it to Longer Marcha #4 from Part 5, from the song *De la Habana,* also in 3-2 clave. Another relative of this marcha is the one Tomasito plays on *Cuida'o en el cachumbambe,* from "El bueno soy yo", the previous Paulito FG album.

More distant relatives are Marchas #3, #5, and #6, already studied here in Part 4. The main feature they have in common is that all are in 3-2 and all feature the open tumba on the downbeat of the 2-side.

Note that although Tomasito uses these marchas in sections which are in 3-2 clave, he thinks of the marchas themselves as starting on the 2-side. Hence, we start the DVD exercise on the 2-side but notate the music so as to show how the rhythms fall in the context of the musical arrangment of *No te lo creas.*

Marcha #10 - DVD Chapters 24 & 25

Clave: **2-3 Rumba**
Tempo: **94**
Album: Paulito FG: Con la conciencia tranquila
Song: *No me puedo enamorar,* 0:11

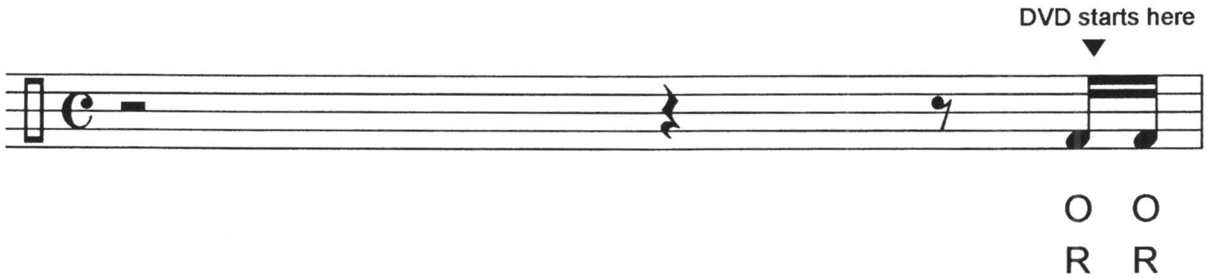

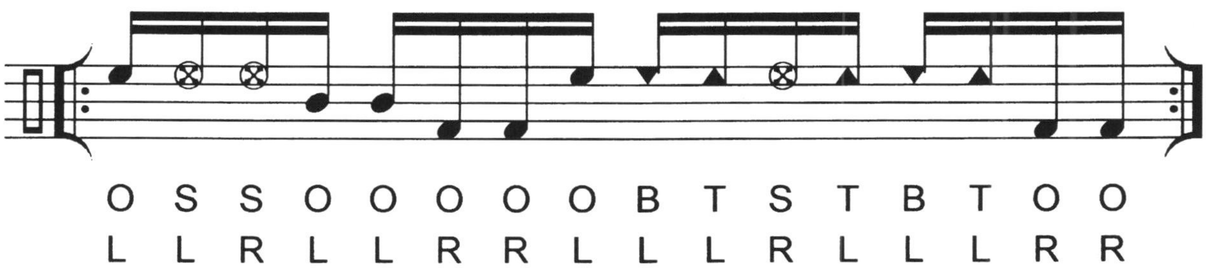

NOTES: This one, which Tomasito calls *marcha con melodía,* is used in the introduction to *No me puedo enamorar*. Variations of it are also used during the mambos of *No te lo creas.* It's often made into a 2-bar pattern by anticipating the initial open tone every other time.

Marchas from Tomasito's Recordings with El Médico de la Salsa

Marcha #11- DVD Chapters 26 & 27

Clave: **2-3 Rumba**
Tempo: **90**
Album: Manolín, el Médico de la Salsa: "El puente" (also on "Jaque mate")
Song: *Yo gocé*

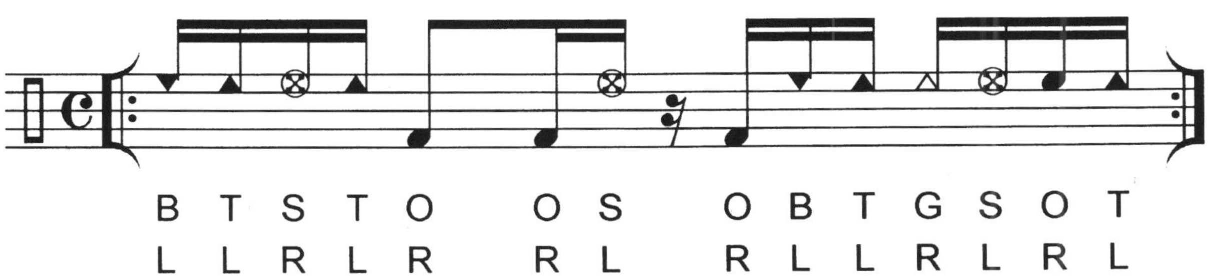

NOTES: Tomasito calls this rhythm *Marcha Apambichao,* meaning that the rhythm is influenced by the Dominican *Apambichao,* a slower tempo merengue variant studied in detail in the Merengue section of Volume II.

PART 5: LONGER MARCHAS

Prior to the 90's almost all conga marchas lasted only one clave, some even half a clave, but as Tomasito and others began to incorporate creative melodic elements into their marchas it was only natural to increase their lengths to allow for more melodic development.

These 2 & 4-clave marchas are too long to use the Step by Step DVD method, but each one still gets two DVD chapters, one at full speed and the other in slow motion. We strongly suggest *completely* mastering the 11 one clave marchas before tackling this section. The longer marchas will be much easier to learn after the new hand patterns introduced in Part 4 are fully assimilated, and if you avail yourself of the DVD, the first 11 can be learned very quickly.

Longer Marchas from Tomasito's Recordings with Paulito FG

Longer Marcha #1 - DVD Chapters 28 & 29

Clave: 2-3 Rumba
Tempo: 92
Album: Paulito FG: Con la conciencia tranquila
Song: *Con la conciencia tranquila,* coro 1, 1:45

O O
R R

O O B T O S O B T S O T O O T
L R L L R L R L L R R L R R L

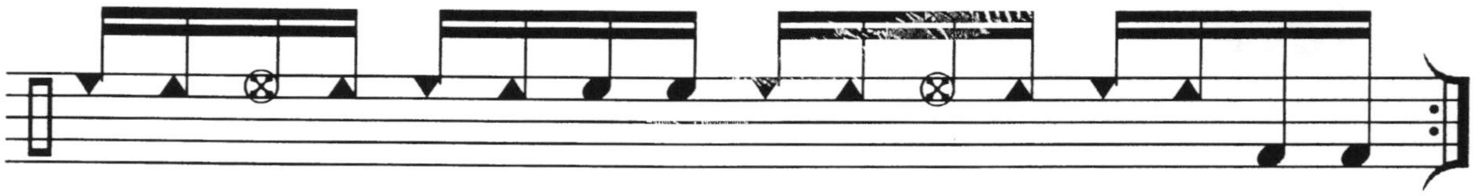

B T S T B T O O B T S T B T O O
L L R L L L R R L L R L L L R R

NOTES: Tomasito calls this a *Marcha Bomba* because of its incorporation of elements from the Puerto Rican Bomba, but he would *not* use this marcha in a Timba Bomba section; its stable groove is more appropriate for coros. If you have the recording, note the relationship to the bassline. The first half of the marcha reinforces the bass and the second half responds to it. Also note that the second half is a standard Salsa marcha except for the last two strokes.

Longer Marcha #2 - DVD Chapters 30 & 31

Clave: 2-3 Rumba
Tempo: 93.5
Album: Paulito FG: Con la conciencia tranquila
Song: *Entre dos amigos,* coro 2, 2:56

B T S G O O G B T S T B T O B
L L R R L L R L L R L L L R L

T O S O O S O O B T S T B T O T
L R L R R L R R L L R L L L R L

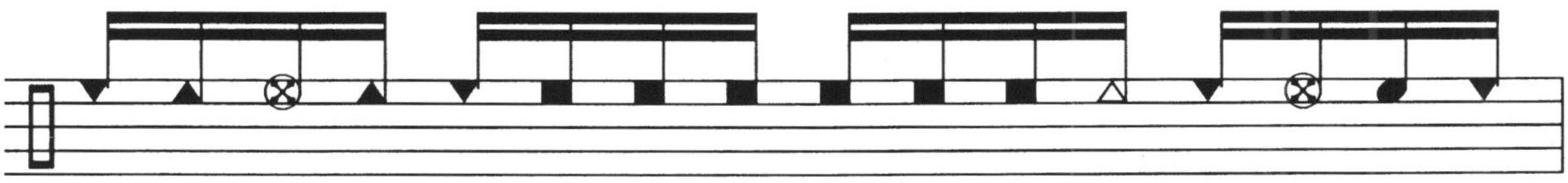

B T S T B M M M M M M G B S O B
L L R L L R L R L R L R L L R L

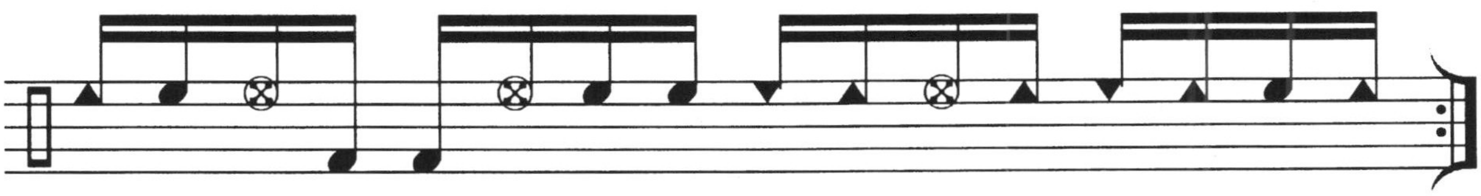

T O S O O S O O B T S T B T O T
L R L R R L R R L L R L L L R L

NOTES: Over the course of rehearsing *Entre dos amigos,* Tomasito gradually developed this into a 4-bar marcha. The final touch came from arranger Juan Ceruto, who suggested adding the two strokes on the middle drum in the first bar. The Paulito group rehearsed as often as 6 times a week and many of their creative arranging ideas were developed in this way. Tomasito says he would not use this marcha in a Bomba section; he suggests using it in fairly uncomplicated coro sections where its melodic subtleties can stand out.

Longer Marcha #3 - DVD Chapters 32 & 33

Clave: 2-3 Rumba
Tempo: 93.5
Album: Paulito FG: Con la conciencia tranquila
Song: A similar but not exact marcha can be found in *No te lo creas,* coro 1, 1:53

NOTES: As can be seen in the analysis of *No te lo creas* in Part 7, this is a pattern which Tomasito uses as a basis for variations, rather than one which is played verbatim each time.

Like the previous marcha, and like Marchas 2 and 7 of Part 4, Tomasito incorporates a series of muffs into his pattern. This distinct 5-stroke figure allows the congas to participate in the overall musical counterpoint. If you have the recording, listen to the way the background singers enter on the fourth of the five muffs, so that two staggered entrances are created. Conversely, the two open tumba tones in the second bar reinforce the coro part. The key point here is that the conguero is not just keeping time, but listening to the other musical elements of the arrangement and accompanying them, reinforcing some parts and counter-balancing others.

Also note the displacement of the "bass-tip-slap-tip" figure to the last 16th of beat 1. Also called *picoteo* or *masacote,* and studied in detail in Volume I, this is probably the most common sequence of hand movements in conga playing. It's almost always played on the downbeats of beats 1 & 3 in traditional conga drumming, but Tomasito will place this figure on any part of any beat.

Longer Marcha #4 - DVD Chapters 34 & 35

Clave: 3-2 Rumba
Tempo: 102
Album: Paulito FG: Con la conciencia tranquila
Song: *De La Habana*, introduction, 0:09

NOTES: *De La Habana*, Paulito FG's most famous song, also contains some of Tomasito's best-known marchas. In fact, many Timba fans in Havana can instantly identify the song just from hearing the conga part. Tomasito combines a normal Timba marcha with elements of both Guaguancó and Batá music. The opening part of the vocal is sung to a true Guaguancó, which may be part of the inspiration for the use of Guaguancó rhythms in the marchas later on. See Voume II for a section on traditional Guaguancó, one of the most influential folkloric rhythms.

As noted earlier, the open tumba tone on the first beat of the 2-side is a common feature of Tomasito's marchas.

Longer Marcha #5 - DVD Chapters 36 & 37

Clave: 3-2 Rumba
Tempo: 102
Album: Paulito FG: Con la conciencia tranquila
Song: *De La Habana*, coro 1, 1:45

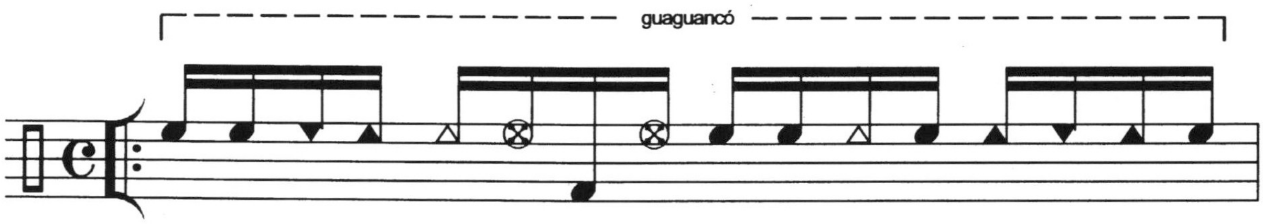

O O B T G S O S O O G O T B T O
L R L L R L R L R L R L R L L R

B T S T G S O S O G O G O S O O
L L R L R L R L R L R L R L R R

NOTES: This variation of the previous marcha uses more open tones for the higher energy montuno section. The other difference is that it's composed entirely of rhythms which Tomasito thinks of as having their origins in folkloric music, whereas the other uses normal marcha patterns in the unbracketed sections.

Photos by Tom Ehrlich

Longer Marcha #6 - DVD Chapters 38 & 39

Clave: 3-2 Rumba
Tempo: 102
Album: Paulito FG: Con la conciencia tranquila
Song: *De La Habana*, coro 2, 2:52

O S O O G O T B T O
R L R L R L R L L R

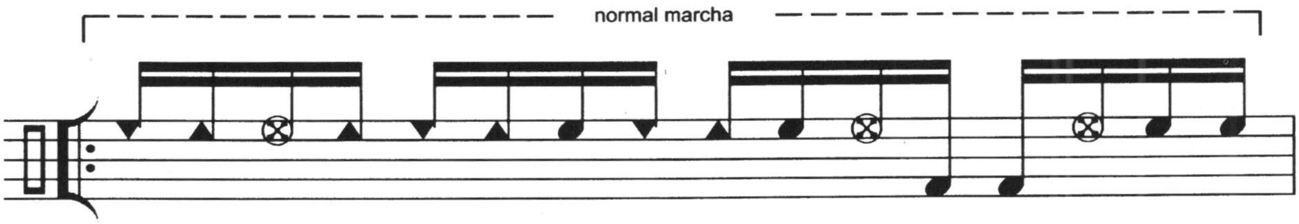

B T S T B T O B T O S O O S O O
L L R L L L R L L R L R R L R R

B T S T B T O S O O G O T B T O
L L R L L L R L R L R L R L L R

NOTES: Although *De La Habana* is in 3-2 from beginning to end, the marchas, and especially this one, are conceived of by Tomasito as starting on the 2-side, hence the notation. When you listen to the recording the logic becomes apparent, as each entrance contains a bloque or fill on the 3-side, resulting in the marcha (and other percussion patterns) usually starting on the 2-side. Mike Gerald points out that this is one of the reasons that 3-2 arrangements tend to sound funkier, as the breaks and fills tend to phrase "across the barlines". It also creates the exciting effect of pleasantly catching the listener off guard by playing a break *after* a section has already begun, as opposed to just before it begins, as one would normally expect in other styles of music. The mix of elements is now marcha and Guaguancó, with the Batá rhythms left behind as this classic arrangement roars to its climactic conclusion.

Longer Marchas from Tomás' Recordings w/ Manolín, el Médico de la Salsa

Manolín, El Médico de la Salsa, is the first Cuban Timba band to have survived outside of the musically-nurturing environment of Havana, where each musician plays in only one group, where each group rehearses many times per week, and where the public knows all the dance moves and understands all the subtleties of the lyrics. In the mid to late 90's Manolín was a massively popular cultural phenomenon in Cuba, filling 90,000 seat sports stadiums, but his lyrics became so politically controversial that he wound up defecting, with almost all of his band intact, to Miami, where he can be heard today, and where he recorded the live double CD, "El Puente". Manolín's original conguero, Alexis "Mipa" Cuesta, was one of the few members who didn't stay with the band, and this is how Tomasito, already in Miami by that time, came to join. It's interesting to compare the conga styles of these two great drummers. Mipa can be heard on Manolín's studio albums and Tomasito on the live disc.

Longer Marcha #7 - DVD Chapters 40 & 41

Clave: 2-3 Rumba
Tempo: 90
Album: Manolín, el Médico de la Salsa: El Puente (original recording on "De Buena Fe")
Song: *No lo comentes*

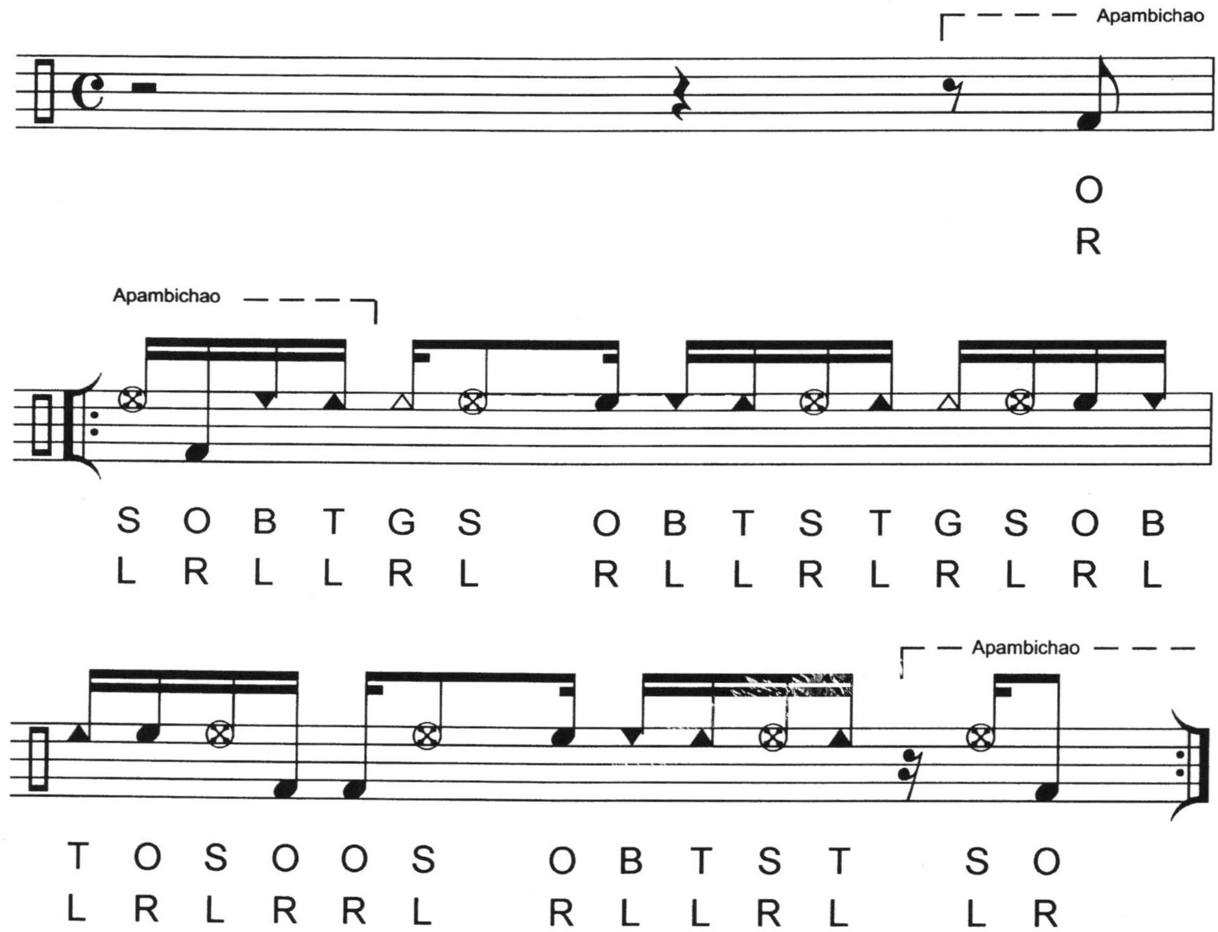

NOTES: Tomasito calls this a *Marcha Apambichao* (see Marcha #11 from the previous section and the Merengue section of Volume II). The bracketed sections show the Apambichao reference. This rhythm, used on a number of Manolín's songs, is barely present in the work of Paulito, just one example of the wide stylistic diversity between the various Timba bands.

Longer Marcha #8 - DVD Chapters 42 & 43

Clave: 2-3 Rumba
Tempo: 90
Album: Manolín, el Médico de la Salsa: El Puente (original recording on "De Buena Fe")
Song: *No lo comentes*

O
R

O O B T G S O B T S T G S O B
R R L L R L R L L R L R L R L

T O S O O S O B T S T S O
L R L R R L R L L R L L R

NOTES: This is a variation on the previous marcha to respond to a change in the bassline.

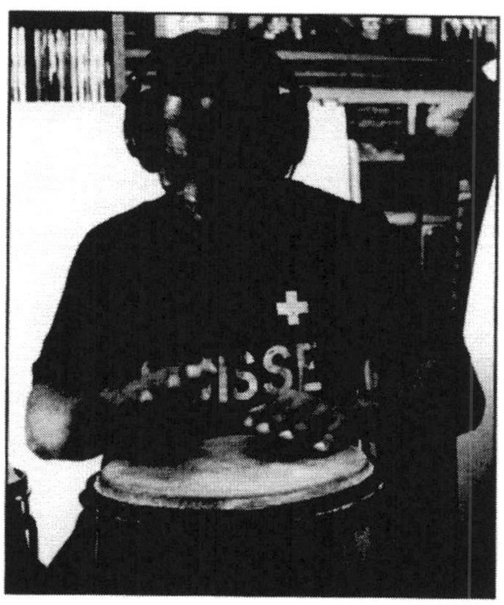

Other Longer Timba Marchas

Here are two additional longer marchas which can be used in a variety of settings. In Parts 6-8 we'll talk more about how to know what type of marcha to use in a given situation and how to invent your own.

Longer Marcha #9 - DVD Chapters 44 & 45

Clave: 2-3 Rumba
Tempo: 92

B T S T O B T O B T S T B T O B
L L R L R L L R L L R L L L R L

T O S O O D O O B T S T B T O T
L R L R R L R R L L R L L L R L

NOTES: Tomasito calls this a *marcha variación*. It could be used in either a normal montuno section or a bomba section and lends itself to variations and improvisations on the part of the conguero.

Longer Marcha #10 - DVD Chapters 46 & 47

Clave: 2-3 Rumba
Tempo: 92

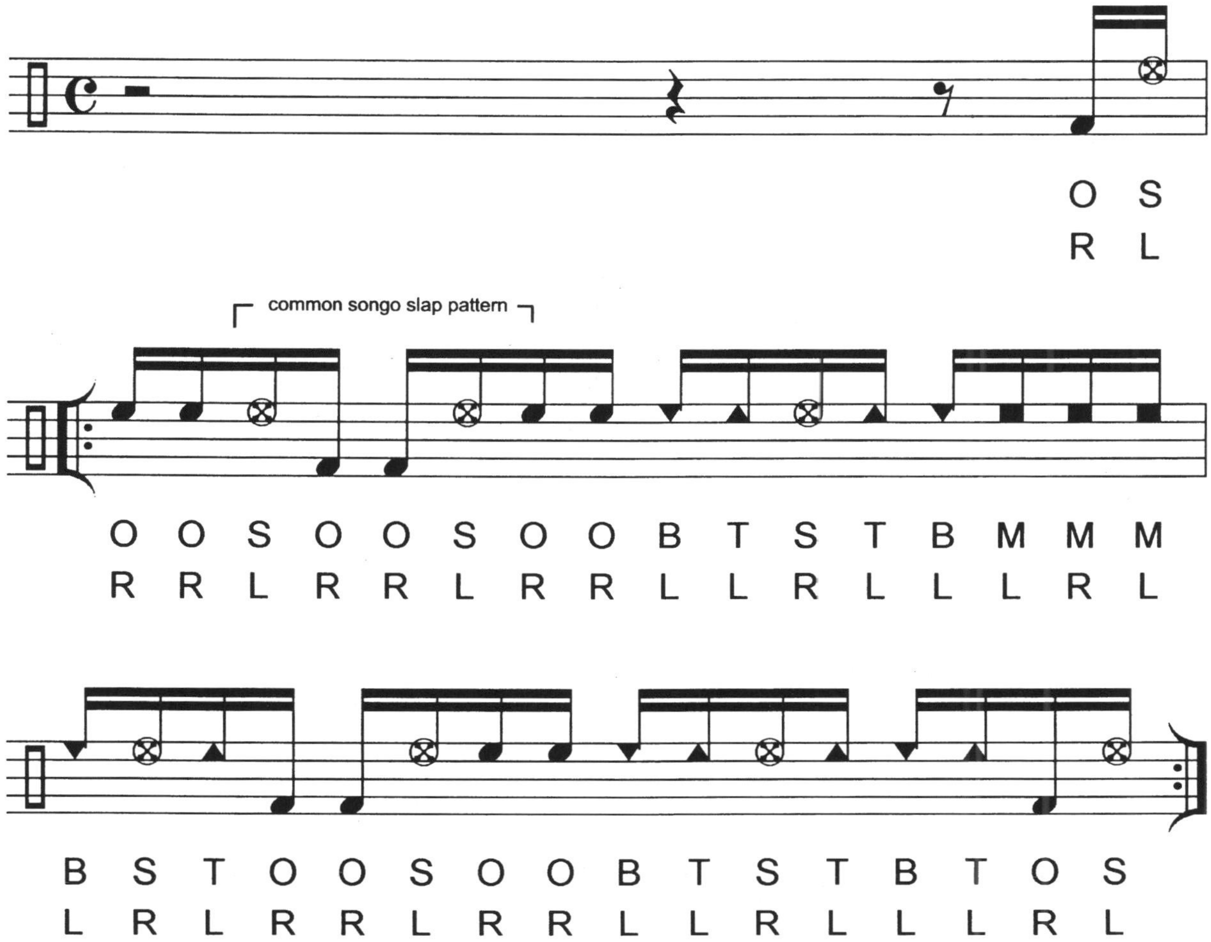

NOTES: Another *marcha variación,* this one isn't used specifically in any of Tomasito's recordings, although it's similar to parts of *Mi tentación* from "Con la Conciencia Tranquila".

This marcha is partially derived from Songo, one of the most important pre-Timba Cuban styles (see Volume II). It's a pattern that's frequently used by conguero Manuel "Manolo" Labarrera (http://manolo.timba.com) of Los Van Van, the group which created the Songo style.

PART 6: PLAYING FULL TIMBA ARRANGEMENTS

When we first started work on these books, the most frequent and emphatic advice we heard was: *"Please don't just write a book full of patterns! You need to explain how to think musically and how to deal with whole arrangements".*

We took this to heart and the rest of this book is devoted to exactly that – learning to play whole arrangements and getting to the point where you can actually play congas in a modern Timba playing situation, whether it be covers of famous arrangements or original creations of your own. When you finish with Parts 6-8 of this book we predict that you'll hear (and play) Timba in a completely new way.

Part 6 begins with an overview called "The Big Picture" and then proceeds to examine the various components of Timba arrangements and to explain how to make the transitions between them. Part 7 is a section by section analysis of DVD Chapter 57, which consists of Tomasito playing the conga part to a complete Timba arrangement. Finally, Part 8 starts with an original piano and bass tumbao, asks you to invent your own marcha, and then gives you Tomasito's solution to the same creative challenge.

The Big Picture

This book and DVD will quickly teach you a large number of conga patterns, but to use them in a band, you'll also need to know which pattern to play when, how to switch between them, and ultimately, how to invent your own creative conga parts. Traditional Salsa and Son are so formulaic that an experienced conguero can often sit in with a new band on a song he's never heard and get through it by playing standard patterns and transitional figures. This is not the case in Timba! By means of hand signals or other visual cues, the rhythm section as a whole can switch between up to a half dozen different types of grooves, or "gears", and these gears and signals vary drastically from group to group! There's also a huge amount of variation and creativity in the work of the great Timba arrangers (see footnote). The result is that it's necessary for percussionists to learn the style of each group and then to learn each song as a unique piece of music, just as the singers and horn players do. However, the learning curve can be greatly shortened by understanding the different types of gears, the conguero's responsibilities in each, and how to smoothly makes the transitions between them.

Later in this section, we'll show specific examples of Tomasito's approach to navigating the gears and transitions of the groups he's played with, but first let's define some of the terms we'll be using.

The important terms and concepts you'll need to understand can be broken into three groups:

1) **Functions of the congas**
2) **Sections of the overall arrangement**
3) **Special modes or gears of the rhythm section**

---

footnote: Here's a partial list of some of the greatest Timba arrangers: Juan Ceruto (of Paulito FG, Issac Delgado, etc.), Joaquín Betancourt (of Issac Delgado and others) David Calzado and Juan Carlos González (of Charanga Habanera), Giraldo Piloto and Yusef Díaz (of Klimax), Luis Bu (of El Médico de la Salsa), Manolito Simonet (of Manolito y su Trabuco), Lázaro Valdés (of Bamboleo), and José Luis Cortés (of NG La Banda). For more on these and others, see www.timba.com.

The terms and their English translations vary greatly from group to group and from player to player. Some rhythm section modes are known only by their hand signals and don't even have official names, so, as always, it's important not to get caught up in semantics.

Functions of the congas

A **marcha**, or **tumbao**, is any repeating rhythm pattern that the conguero or other rhythm section member plays to keep time.

A **bloque**, or break, is a short and exciting rhythmic figure that the conguero plays in unison with the other percussionists, (and sometimes the bass, piano and/or horns), at various key points in the arrangement. Timba has a lot more bloques than Salsa, and they tend to be more complex and creative. Bloques can come during any section. Some groups, such as Bamboleo, have numbered bloques which can be signaled by hand and inserted into any arrangement, but most groups, like Paulito FG and Manolín, compose specific bloques for each arrangement.

Fills are like bloques, except that they're played by only one player, and usually improvised. They can be added during the marcha to add excitement and to respond to other instruments, or during sections where the conguero would otherwise be laying out, such as the Pedal section. In the basic marcha gear, the fills usually fall within the 16th note groove, but in Pedal, Songo, and mambo sections, triplets and folkloric polyrhythms are fair game for the conguero. Fills are rare in Bomba gear, where the top priority is laying down a heavy groove. The term **"efectos"** is used more loosely and can refer to both prearranged and improvised figures.

Laying out should not be overlooked! What you don't play is just as important as what you do play. For example, in the "pedal" gear of the Paulito FG group, the conguero is expected to stop his marcha. Later in this chapter Tomasito demonstrates various ways to make this transition.

A modern Timba rhythm section seldom stays in the same gear for much more than 8 measures and the conguero needs to be constantly alert to navigate the many transitions. These fall into two categories: those that line up with the changes within the overall arrangement itself and, much more difficult, those that occur *within* the same section of the arrangement. This latter type of gear-shifting is one of the keys to mastering the art of playing congas in Timba.

Sections of the Overall Arrangement

The **preview** section, if there is one, gives a brief taste of a coro from later in the song before the beginning of the arrangement. These are very common in concerts, but also sometimes occur on studio recordings (for example, *¿Y San Toma qué?*, from "Con la Conciencia Tranquila").

The **introduction** (introducción) is an instrumental section featuring the horns and/or the keyboards. It can sometimes return at the end of the song as a **coda**, or even during the cuerpo, as it does in *No te lo creas* (see Part 7). Arrangers take a lot of liberties in these sections and the conga parts have to be worked out on a case by case basis.

The **cuerpo**, or "body", or "head", is the main song form that the lead vocalist sings at the beginning of the recording, usually punctuated by the horns. It's almost always the mellowest and most melodic part of the arrangement and the conguero plays much as he would in a Salsa arrangement, although sometimes even in the cuerpo a special marcha is invented to fit to the song. Like any popular song, the cuerpo can have a variety of sections and each section within the cuerpo can have a different marcha (see Part 7 for such an example in *No te lo creas).*

The **puente**, or **bridge** section is a brief transition featuring the horns which leads from the cuerpo to the rest of the arrangement. This is the key dividing point of all Timba arrangements, as well as those of most other styles of Cuba, Puerto Rico and the Dominican Republic. Sometimes all of the sections described so far are lumped together and simply called the Cuerpo and those which follow the **Montuno section**.

Here, as so frequently happens when trying to describe Latin music with words, we get into very tricky semantic territory. "*Montuno*" is a term with many meanings. Outside of Cuba it's a very common name for the pianist's tumbao. In Timba, it can be one of several coro sections with distinct tumbaos. In this case the sections are called "Montuno 1", "Montuno 2", etc., but "Montuno section" could also be taken to mean the entire second half of the arrangement, including all of its coros, mambos and other sections. This use of the term comes from the traditional Cuban style of Son Montuno. Most of the musical styles of Cuba, Puerto Rico and the Dominican Republic share this most basic division of each arrangement into a mellower, more melodic opening and a higher energy, more danceable conclusion.

Each individual montuno section can have its own chord progression, during which **coro** and **mambo** sections alternate and are sometimes separated by other special sections.

The **coro** section features a call and response between the **coros** of the backup singers and the **guías** (previously called **pregones**)of the lead vocalist. There are usually several coro sections in each arrangement. As in Salsa, the conguero plays a steady marcha which is more energetic than the cuerpo, but in Salsa, that pattern is almost always the standard Salsa pattern taught in Volume I. In Timba, coro sections use a wide range of marchas, and in some cases, a unique marcha is created for just one coro. Tomasito has created many such marchas and says that his approach is to listen to the whole arrangement, and the bass in particular, and try to find a marcha which fits melodically into the overall texture. Timba arrangers spend a great deal of time and effort making their coro sections as interesting and creative as possible, which sometimes leads to unusual asymmetrical patterns between the backup and lead vocalists. With the Cuban public, the coros, and their tumbaos, frequently play the most important role in determining whether a song will be a big hit. After a year or two, groups will frequently drop the cuerpo of a popular number and play only the coros and mambos in concert.

The **mambo** section features the horns, but is also the section where the conguero has the most freedom to add soloistic material and polyrhythms. In traditional Salsa, the vocalists lay out and the horns play a figure that usually lasts 4 or 8 bars and is then repeated 2 or 4 times. In Timba, all bets are off! The horns, coros, and lead vocals can be combined in a myriad of clever combinations and the lengths and phrasing are also fair game for the arranger's creativity. The conguero's marcha becomes more active and dynamic when the horns enter, and the quantity and intensity of fills increases. In fact, the conga player is *expected* to play at least one fiery fill during each mambo, and it needs to fit in not only with the horn parts, but with the fills of the other percussionists. In the music of Paulito FG, the drummer usually plays a fill just before the halfway point of the mambo and the conguero plays one just after it.

The **motivo** section, if there is one, is a breakdown designed to introduce a particularly interesting tumbao, usually played in unison by the pianist's left hand and the bass. The conguero usually lays out except for fills during this section, although he may also play a soft, unobtrusive marcha. An example of a motivo section can be found at 3:03 of *¿Y ahora qué?*, the second track of "Con la Conciencia Tranquila".

Solo sections feature individual instrumentalists, either with or without coros.

Champola sections are like Dixieland Jazz. Each horn plays a separate part, some improvised. The bass, piano and usually congas lay out to showcase the overlapping horn parts.

Breakdowns occur more often in concert than on studio recordings. The band suddenly drops way down in volume, allowing the singer to talk to the crowd, sing a prolonged improvisation without coros, and/or introduce a new coro. This frequently involves encouraging the crowd to sing the coro, during which the band will stop completely for a measure except for the kick drum and/or the clave. A rare studio example of a breakdown can be found at 4:02 of *¿Y San Toma qué?* from "Con la conciencia tranquila" by Paulito FG.

The **coda** section concludes the arrangement.

Special Modes or Gears of the Rhythm Section

In almost all types of music, the percussionists are expected to understand the overall form of the arrangement and change their parts accordingly when each transition occurs, but in Timba the rhythm section also changes gears *within* these sections. Gears such as **Bomba**, **Pedal** and **Songo con efectos** *can* come at the transition point from one section of the arrangement to the next, but more often than not they come by means of hand signals *during* coros and mambos. These modes are integrally connected with the dancers. For example, Tomasito explains that the gear he calls *Songo con efectos* was introduced by the Paulito FG group after the recording of "Con la conciencia tranquila". The band began to experiment with it and when they could see that the dancers liked it and would change their dancing in sync with it, they began to incorporate it as a regular gear in their performances. During Pedal and Bomba sections, the dancers break apart and dance *despelote* style, with arms in the air and wild improvisational gyrations.

The band can mix these gears in various orders and the transitions are usually cued by hand signals from the singer and/or musical director. Different Timba groups have different gears, different names for them and different hand signals, and, as Tomasito's account indicates, the gears are always changing and evolving, just like the changing styles of dance.

The **Bomba** gear has its roots in the Puerto Rican *Bomba Sicá*, but has evolved into a uniquely Cuban groove. Most Timba bands incorporate Bomba sections into their style and both Paulito and Manolín make heavy use of it. After aggressive pickups of the snare drum, the bass player stops playing time and plays funky Batá-influenced figures by sliding the palm down the low string. The space vacated by the bass tumbao is filled by aggressive percussion featuring a steady campana, backbeat snare on the 2-side, hihat, toms, and heavy conga marchas with lots of open tones. The dancers go wild and the energy builds up in preparation for the next transition, which is most often back to normal marcha by means of a bloque. The conguero's job in Bomba is to play a strong, steady marcha with open tones which complement the toms and the bass slides. As explained above, the rhythm section can go in or out of a Bomba groove at any point without waiting for the next transition in the overall arrangement. The most common length for a Bomba section is 8 bars, but they can last as few as 4 or as many as 16 bars.

Also unique to Timba is the dramatic **Pedal** gear. The bass plays a series of long, majestic "pedal tones". The drums play clave and kick drum. The campana plays sparsely, accenting the 3-side of the clave, and, at least in the Paulito band's approach, the congas stop playing time entirely. Each pedal section has a specific bloque, played by all the members of the rhythm section except the pianist , the only musician to keep playing a normal tumbao and the pricipal timekeeper in Pedal. Between the hits of the bloque the percussionists play improvised fills. Tomasito describes the Pedal section as being one of the emotional climaxes of the arrangement.

Songo con efectos was introduced by the Paulito band in 1998, after the recording of "Con la Conciencia Tranquila". Like Bomba gear, the rhythm section can go into this mode in the middle of a coro or mambo already in progress, but the flavor of the groove is quite different. The bass drops out except for a sparse predetermined figure. As in Pedal gear, the drummer plays clave and kick drum, and both the drummer and the bongocero stop their bell patterns – but the conguero, instead of dropping out, as in Pedal, moves to the forefront and plays loosely around an aggressive Songo *Bota* marcha. The other percussionists respond improvisationally. In Bomba the emphasis is on laying down a steady, aggressive groove; any fills or variations fall within the 16th note subdivisions. Songo con efectos is much more improvised and polyrhythmic. See Volume II for more on the Songo roots of this gear and a detailed appendix with multiple written examples of its use in the Paulito group.

A gear seldom used by Paulito FG, but common in the music of Issac Delgado, is the **piano tumbao** gear, in which *everything* drops out except for piano, clave, kick drum, and voices.

Thus, in "the big picture", the success of the torrid Timba groove is heavily dependent on the conguero, who must be constantly switching between up to six different gears. Each requires a different style of playing, and each requires close attention to the other instruments in order to respond to what's going on in that particular performance of that particular arrangement. There's lot of room for soloing and creative variations, but you have to know where and you have to be alert at all times to navigate the many transitions.

One last word of warning: we can't overstress the complete irrelevance of semantics! All of these definitions and concepts must be taken loosely because the Timba genre is still in a creative growth spurt and still changing. Timba arrangements vary drastically – from group to group and even from song to song. The terminology also varies from group to group. *Trying to come up with a rigid system to explain this music defeats the flexibility and creativity that make it so great in the first place.* We strongly recommend that the student become familiar with the entire Timba repertoire and especially the recordings cited in the notes for each pattern. Musical terms and theories come from great music – not the other way around. Live with the great Timba recordings and when you create your own, think creatively, not dogmatically!

The Marcha Gear

Like *"montuno"*, the term *"marcha"* has several meanings. Up to this point we've used it to mean the repeating rhythm patterns of the conguero and other percussionists. But "marcha" is also the "normal" rhythm section gear that the band returns to from the special gears such as Pedal and Bomba. The conguero has a lot of leeway to vary the marcha he uses in this gear. Here's a listening exercise to help develop the skill of tastefully varying your marchas.

Listening Exercise

Choose a Timba recording and focus on the voices and horns instead of the repeating patterns of the congas. Now listen to the spaces in between the phrases of the melodic instruments and note that the conguero chooses fills and variations, as well as the open tones and slaps of the marchas, so as to balance the melodic phrases. Cuban music is like a conversation, taking place on many levels simultaneously. As you get used to listening in this way, the dense texture will become much more orderly and logical and you'll begin to understand how to appropriately vary your own patterns as a conguero.

To further improve your listening skills, we recommend the internet article, "Conversations in Timba", at: http://conversations.timba.com.

Bloques within Marchas

One of the defining characteristics of the Timba style is the frequent use of exciting and creative bloques at unexpected places within the arrangement. Bloques are worked out in advance and played together by several members of the rhythm section. When they occur during the pedal section it's easier for the conguero, who isn't responsible for keeping time at that point -- it's just a matter of learning the bloque and playing it. But bloques also occur quite often during the other sections of the arrangement. In these cases the conguero must interrupt his marcha to play the bloque and then resume keeping time again afterwards. Here's an example of a bloque within a marcha from the cuerpo of the title track of "Con la Conciencia Tranquila". If you have the recording, it occurs at 1:06.

B T S T B T OOOOO O OOOOO O O
L L R L L L RRLLR L RRLLR L R

etc.

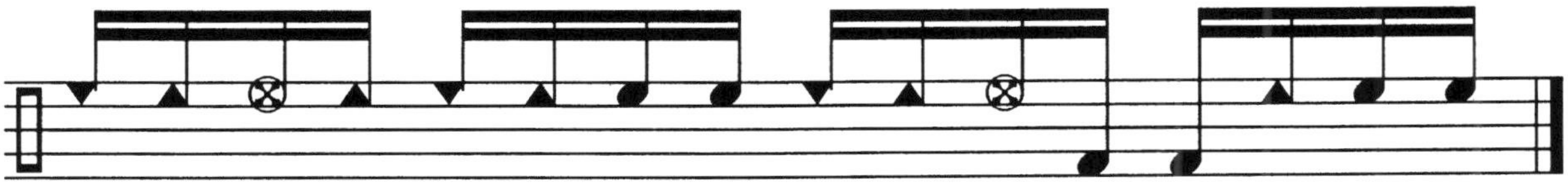

B T S T B T O O B T S O O T O O
L L R L L L R R L L R R R L R R

More on Bloques

For more on bloques, refer to the internet article, "The Bloques of Charanga Habanera", at:

http://bloques.timba.com

Note: The "gear" descriptions that follow refer most directly to the style of Tomasito's first group, Paulito FG y su Élite. While all Timba groups use the concept of gears, the gears themselves vary somewhat from group to group. As we said before, it's necessary to learn the style of each Timba group, including your own!

The Pedal Gear

The Pedal gear in Timba is an example of addition by subtraction. In the Paulito FG band's approach to Pedal, the bass, the bongocero's campana bell and the congas all stop playing straight time and yet the excitement level of the music rises dramatically. Getting in and out of the Pedal section with flair and energy is absolutely critical to Timba conga playing.

Getting into the Pedal Section

All you really have to do is stop, but you need to do it in an exciting way, sometimes in pre-planned coordination with the other percussionists and sometimes not. Here are six ways to make the transition from the marcha to the Pedal section:

Pedal Entrance #1 – DVD Chapter 48

Pedal Section

Pedal Entrance #2 – DVD Chapter 49

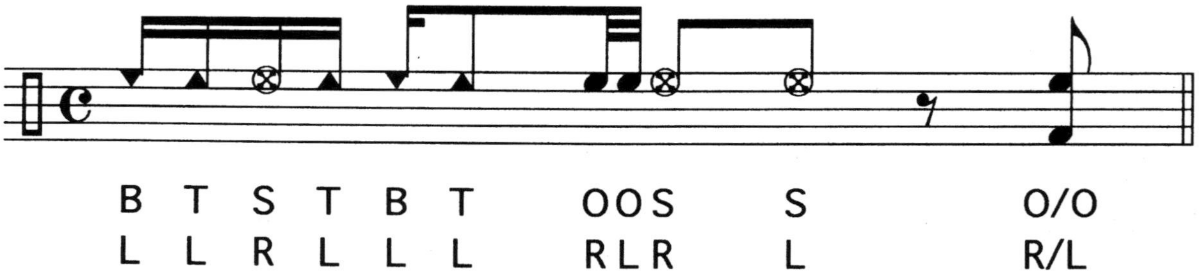

Pedal Section

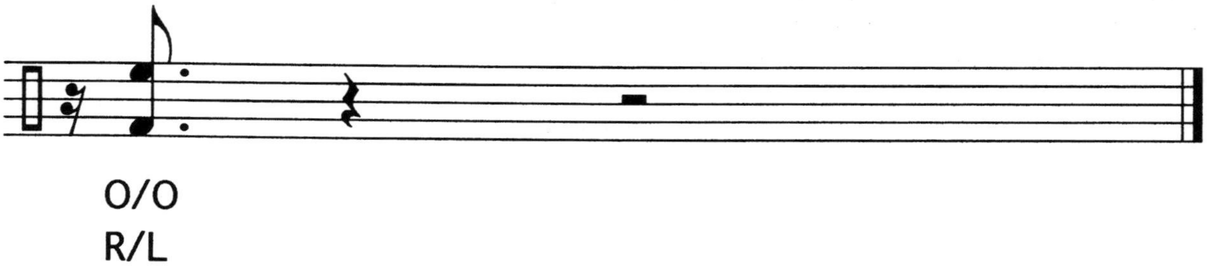

Pedal Entrance #3 – DVD Chapter 50

B T S T B T OOS S O/O

L L R L L L RLR L R/L

Pedal Section

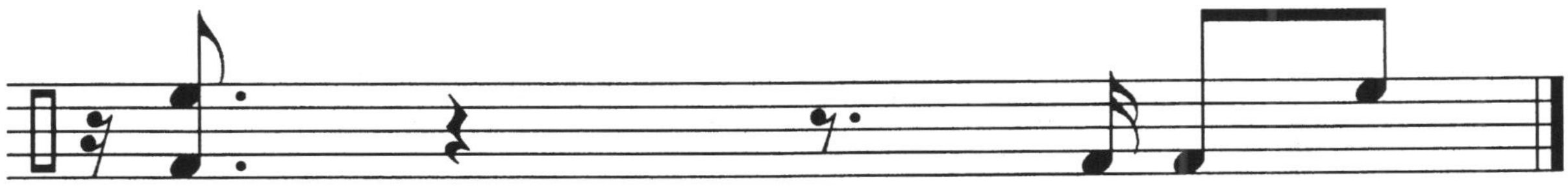

O/O O O O

R/L R R L

Pedal Entrance #4 – DVD Chapter 51

B T S T B T O O O O O O O S S O O

L L R L L L R L R L R L R L R R L

Pedal Section

Pedal Entrance #5 – DVD Chapter 52

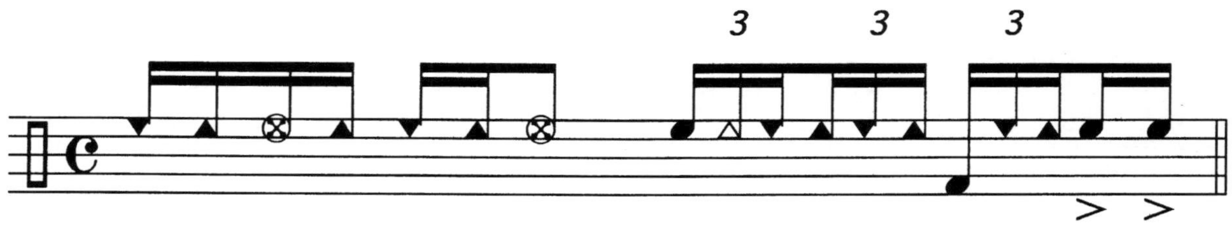

B T S T B T S O G B T B T O B T O O
L L R L L L R R L R R L L R L L R L

Pedal Section

Pedal Entrance #6 – DVD Chapter 53

B T S T B T O O B T S T O B T S
L L R L L L R R L L R L R L L R

Pedal Section

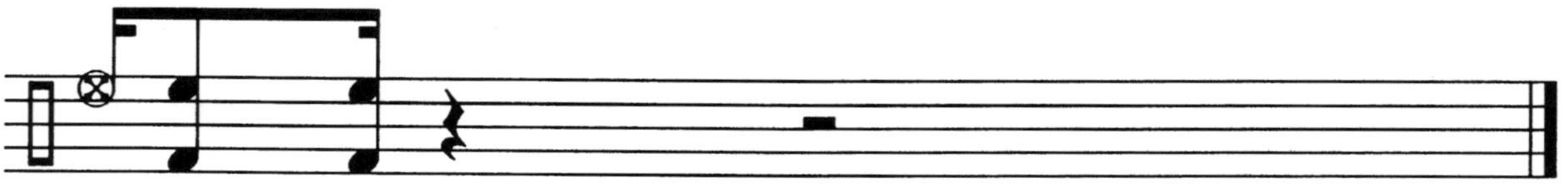

S O/O O/O
L L/R L/R

During the Pedal Section:

In between any pre-composed bloques, the conguero is free to lay out or to improvise tastefully. Tomasito likes to use his elbow to create harmonics during these sections, and he frequently uses folkloric rhythms, even 6/8 triplet figures, in his fills. Here are two examples:

Pedal Improvisation #1 – DVD Chapter 54

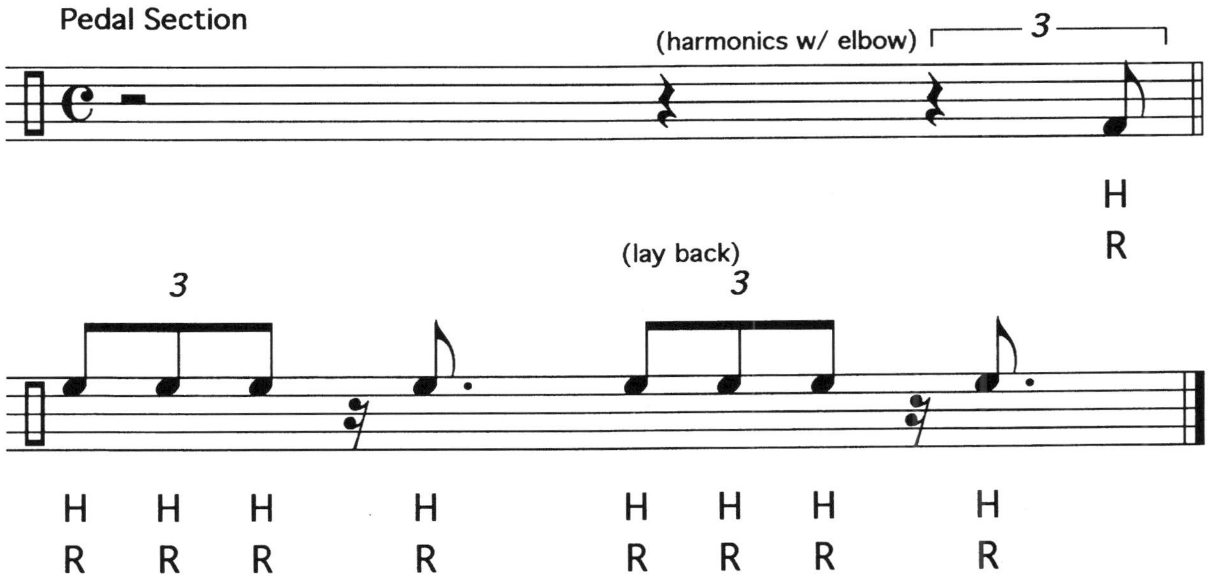

Pedal Improvisation #2 – DVD Chapter 55

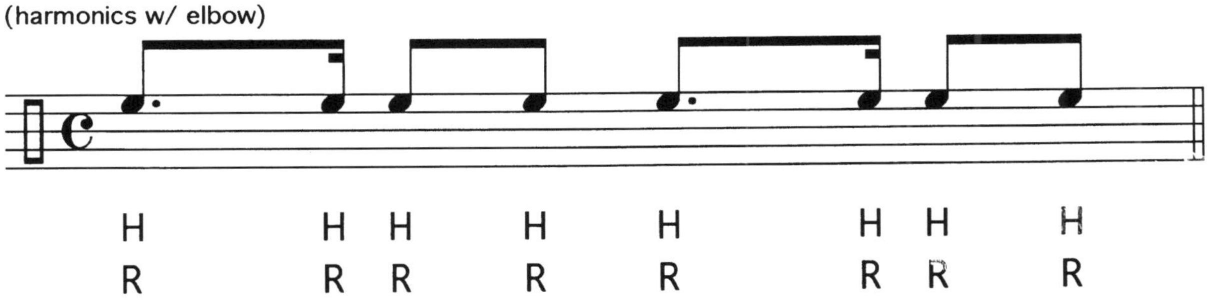

A Complete Pedal Section

DVD Chapter 56 demonstrates a complete Pedal section from Paulito FG's *"No te lo creas"*, starting at 2:54. It shows the transition from the marcha to the Pedal section, the pre-composed bloques and finally the transition back into the next marcha.

Complete Pedal Section – DVD Chapter 56

Clave: 2-3 Rumba
Tempo: 94
Album: Paulito FG: Con la conciencia tranquila
Song: *No te lo creas*, 2:54

O S S O O O O O B T S T B T O O
L L R L L R R L L L R L L L R R

last time

O S S O O O O O B T S T O B T S
L L R L L R R L L L R L R L L R

Pedal Section Begins - 2:54

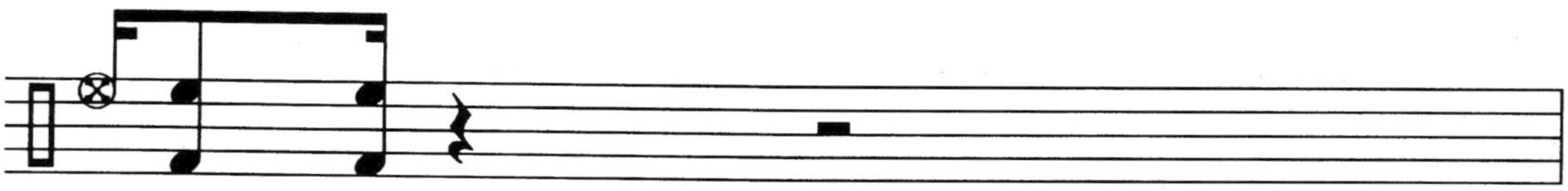

S O/O O/O
L R/L R/L

O O O B O/O
R L R R R/L

The Bomba Gear

The bassist makes the most dramatic change in the Bomba gear – abandoning the normal bass tumbao for a series of funky hand slides down the lowest string. The 3 percussionists lay down a relentless groove with a minimum of frills. The bongocero plays straight campana bell, the drummer plays a steady ride with lots of toms and some snare, and the conguero plays an aggressive marcha with lots of open tones. In Parts 3 & 4 we note which marchas are appropriate for use in Bomba. More examples of Bomba marchas can be found in Part 7.

The Songo con Efectos Gear

Tomasito & Co. introduced this new rhythm section gear in their live performances of 1998 after the recording of "Con la conciencia". Rare live tapes from 1998 can be found in Cuba and some have made their way to the US and Europe. They're well worth seeking out! Tomás, as well as drummer Yoel Páez and bassist Joel Domínguez, left the Paulito group before the next CD, "Una vez más...por amor" (ProMusic CDP-013), which contains a few examples of the Songo con Efectos gear. One can be found at 4:39 of the second track, *Una vez más*, which was originally called *La última bala* and recorded as a Cuban radio demo by the 1998 band. This highly improvisational gear starts with a rapid flourish of percussion into the downbeat of "1". The bass drops out entirely except for a sparse predetermined riff. The bongocero stops his campana bell pattern and improvises, as does the drummer, in addition to keeping the time with clave and kick drum. The congas improvise very loosely around the Songo Bota marcha (see Volume II). This gear, the subject of a special appendix in Volume II, was developing rapidly throughout 1998. Had the band stayed together, Songo con efectos and other new gears would no doubt have continued to evolve. Keep that in mind in your own creative work!

PART 7: PERFORMANCE AND ANALYSIS OF A COMPLETE TIMBA ARRANGEMENT

DVD Chapter 57

To see how everything we've learned fits together in real life, we asked Tomasito to play the complete conga part to one of the arrangements he recorded in Cuba.

Start by watching the DVD chapter a number of times as if it were a piece of music written for solo conga, rather than the conga part to a band arrangement played out of context. The succession of contrasting melodic marchas and the embellishments and transitions between them is musically interesting – enough so to hold your attention even without the parts of the other instruments and voices. Many of the marchas and bloques will sound familiar because we've already studied them earlier in the course as individual exercises.

Next, follow along with just the headings of the 19 sections of the analysis which begins below, listening to the general differences between the different parts of the Cuerpo, the coros and mambos, the Pedal and Bomba sections, and so on.

If you don't already have it, we highly recommend acquiring the actual recording, *"No te lo creas"*, from Paulito FG's "Con la conciencia tranquila" on Nueva Fania Records. It can be easily purchased on the internet at www.amazon.com, www.timba.com, www.descarga.com, and many other sites, as well as some of the larger record stores. This will allow you to follow along with the more specific comments in the analysis and also to compare the DVD performance with the one on the CD, allowing you to hear which parts of the arrangement Tomasito plays similarly each time (a surprisingly large amount) and which parts he leaves open to variation.

The Cuerpo Section

SECTION 1: INTRODUCTION (0:00 to 0:11): Tomasito begins with Marcha #8 from Part 4 (DVD Chapters 20 & 21). This same distinctive pattern will return two more times -- when the introduction is repeated between the two halves of the cuerpo, and during the puente section which leads out of the cuerpo.

It's a very catchy conga part, but what type of musical thinking led Tomasito to construct it as he did? The first order of business was to fit in with the Puerto Rican Bomba Sicá rhythm upon which the introduction is based. This accounts for the two pairs of open tumba tones. The next step was to fit in musically with the overall arrangement. The theme of the introduction is a conversation between a repeating figure in the keyboards and the horns, who alternate between rhythmic stabs and short melodic phrases. The open tones of the congas echo the rhythm of the keyboard, while the repeated slap figure forms a counter-rhythm.

Let's pause to take a quick look at the overall form of the beginning of this track. After the introduction just discussed, the Cuerpo begins. It has an A section and a B section. Then, at 0:51, the intro, Cuerpo A, and Cuerpo B are repeated with different lyrics. Then the introduction seems to comes back for a third time, but the horns are different and lead climactically from the Cuerpo to the Montuno section. This type of section is called the *puente* or "bridge". So up to this point we have Intro, Cuerpo A, Cuerpo B, Intro, Cuerpo A, Cuerpo B, and Puente. Tomasito uses the special marcha just discussed for the Intro/Puente and another (see Section 3 on the next page) for Cuerpo B, and he plays these more or less note-for-note every time, but the Cuerpo A section has no special marcha. He plays a basic salsa marcha and improvises variations as he feels them, responding to the lead vocal and the other instruments.

SECTION 2: CUERPO A (0:12 to 0:31): The basic marcha is:

B T S T B T O O B T S T B T O O
L L R L L L R R L L R L L L R R

The variations are different each time and different between various performaces of the song. Here are several:

Cuerpo A -- Variation #1

B T S T B T O O B T S T O S O O
L L R L L L R R L L R L R L R R

Cuerpo A -- Variation #2

B T S T B T O O B T S T O O O O
L L R L L L R R L L R L R L L R

Cuerpo A -- Variation #3

B T S T B T O O T B S T B T O O

L L R L L L R L R L R L L L R R

Cuerpo A -- Variation #4 *(this is from 0:22 of the original CD and is not found on the DVD performance, a further indication of the improvisational nature of this section.)*

B T S T O O O O B T S T O S O O

L L R L R L L R L L R L R L R R

SECTION 3: CUERPO B – (0:32 to 0:51): This section has its own distinct marcha, taught in DVD Chapters 22 & 23, and played without variations. Note how perfectly the two open tumba notes fill the open spaces of the melody.

B T S T B T O S O G O S S O O O

L L R L L L R L R L R R L R R L

The next three sections are very similar to the first three, differing only in the lyrics and the improvised parts of the accompaniment. The conga marchas already shown are repeated.

SECTION 4: REPEAT OF INTRO (0:51 to 0:56): (like Section 1)

SECTION 5: CUERPO A2 (2nd time) (0:57 to 1:17): (like Section 2)

SECTION 6: CUERPO B2 (2nd time) (1:17 to 1:36): (like Section 3)

SECTION 7: PUENTE ("bridge") (1:37 to 1:42): Because the Puente is based on the introduction, the congas return to the opening marcha. Tomasito plays a nice improvised fill to make the transition into the Puente.

end of Cuerpo B

B T S T B T O O O O O O O O S
L L R L L L R L L R L R L R L

Puente

S B T S S O O S S O O/S S O O S
R L L R L R R L R L L/R L R R L

This particular Puente is a "bridge" in two different senses. Like all Puentes, it marks the transition from the Cuerpo to the Montuno section, but in this case it also smooths out the transition from the Cuerpo's 3-2 clave to the 2-3 clave used for the rest of the arrangement. Many Cuban groups, such as Los Van Van and Charanga Habanera, think nothing of "jumping" from one clave to the other without adding a bar of 2/4 to avoid playing one side of the clave twice in succession, but Paulito's arranger, Juan Ceruto, usually prefers not to break the flow of the clave. In this rare exception, instead of using a bar of 2/4, he simply inserts a section using the clave-neutral Bomba rhythm between the 3-2 and 2-3 sections.

The Montuno Section

SECTION 8: PIANO TUMBAO (1:43 to 1:53):

One of the great advancements of Timba is the idea of making each piano tumbao a unique musical creation -- a "hook" by which the song can be identified and which sticks in the listener's ear. This one, played by the great Sergio Noroña, is particularly memorable and to call attention to it, the bass drops out and the congas play an inobtrusive time-keeping marcha, but even here Tomasito comes up with a special marcha with an unusual twist.

At the end of the section the whole rhythm section plays a bloque to introduce the first coro. Note that the left hand plays two consecutive strokes in the rapid embellishment figures that Tomasito uses here and also in the previous example. This is an application of drumming rudiments to hand percussion and is covered in detail in Volume I of this series.

This entire section is written out on the next page.

SECTION 8: PIANO TUMBAO (1:43 to 1:53): (See notes on previous page).

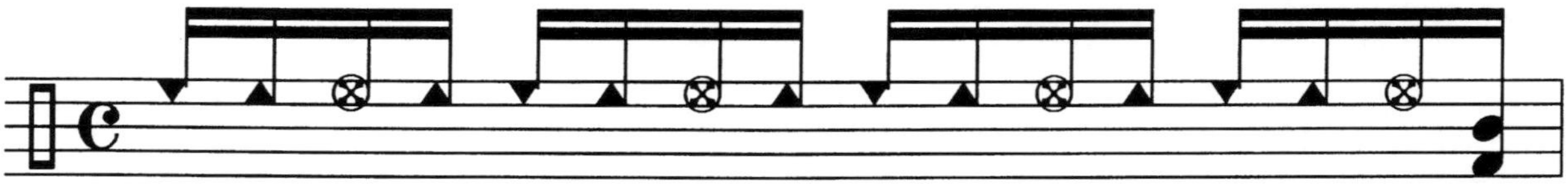

B T S T B T S T B T S T B T S O/O
L L R L L L R L L L R L L L R L/R

O/O B S T B T S T B T S T B T S O/O
L/R L R L L L R L L L R L L L R L/R

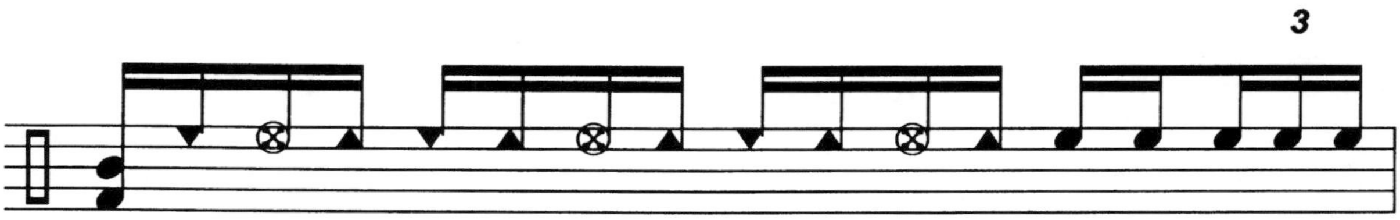

O/O B S T B T S T B T S T O O O O O
L/R L R L L L R L L L R L R L R L L

O B T O O O O O O M M
R L L R R L L R L R L

SECTION 9: MONTUNO 1 – CORO 1 (1:54 to 2:33): This section consists of two 4-bar coros, each followed by a 4-bar *guía* (vocal improvisation by the lead singer). Tomasito plays loosely here, with different variations each time. Many of the ideas, such as the muff tone figure at the beginning are very similar to Longer Marcha #3 from Part 5.

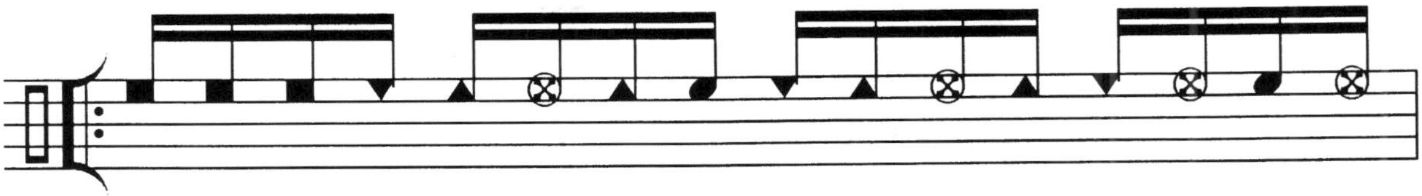

M M M B T S T O B T S T B S O S
R L R L L R L R L L R L L L R L

O O S O O S O O B T S T B T M M
R R L R R L R R L L R L L L R L

At the end of the first coro (2:02), a bloque briefly interrupts the marcha, a very common occurence in Timba. Because the bloque runs over into the next bar, Tomasito can't start the next phrase with the muff tone figure, so he plays a normal marcha for the first two beats before falling back into the previous cycle.

marcha

M M M B T S O O B T S T B S O S
R L R L L R R R L L R L L L R L

bloque - - - - - - - - - - - - - - -

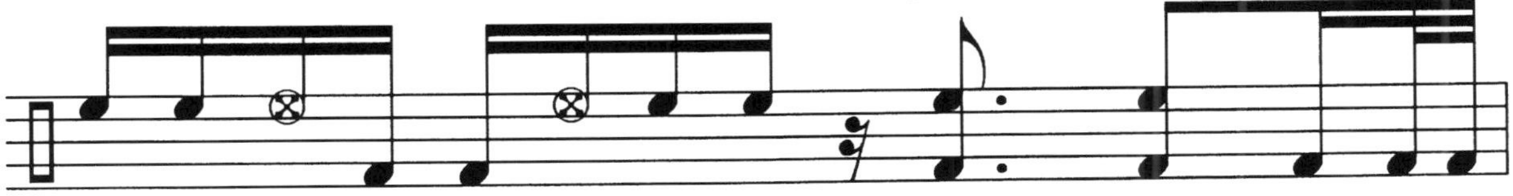

O O S O O S O O O/O O/O O O O
R R L R R L R R R/L R/L R R L

- - - **marcha**

O T S T B T O O B T S T B S O S
R L R L L L R R L L R L L L R L

SECTION 10: MAMBO 1 (2:34 to 2:53): As usual, the entrance of the horns is accompanied by an increase in energy and improvisation from the percussionists and Tomasito plays much more freely in his marchas and fills. In this case, he brings in the third conga and plays variations using all three drums. For example:

O S S O O O O O B T S T G S O B
R L R L L R R L R L R L R L R L

T O S O O S O O B T S T G S G S
L R L R R L R R L L R L R L R L

Like virtually all Timba mambo sections, this one is loaded with fiery fills, or *recursos*. The drummer, Yoel Páez, ushers the section in and plays another recurso at 2:41, which Tomasito answers, at 2:45, with this figure:

O B S S S B T B T S S B T B T S S B T B T S S B
L L R R L R L R L R L R L R L R L R L R L R L R

return to marcha

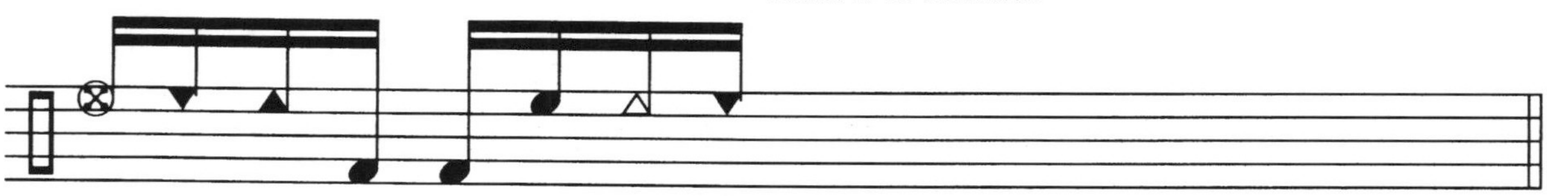

S B T O O O G B
R L L R R L R L

Tomasito plays one more fill at 2:53 to lead into the next section.

SECTION 11: CORO 2/PEDAL (2:54 to 3:04): As explained earlier, the conguero's responsibility in the type of Pedal section used by Paulito FG is to stop playing a marcha and to play whatever bloques have been worked out in advance with the other percussionists. The rest of the space can be silent or contain harmonics or other effects. These are improvised, as you can hear from comparing the DVD performance to the CD performance. Hopefully you're now starting to get a feel for which parts of an arrangement must be worked out in advance and memorized and which can and should be improvised. Here are the essential bloques of this particular Pedal section:

Note that 2:54 is also the beginning of the Coro 2 section. Pedal sections are frequently used to create a dramatic entrance for a particularly interesting new coro or piano tumbao. Tomasito refers to Pedal sections as being among the key emotional climaxes of an arrangement.

SECTION 12: MONTUNO 2 – CONTINUATION OF CORO 2 (3:05 to 3:24): After the bloque, the rhythm section returns to normal marcha gear and Coro 2 continues for two more cycles. This coro is a great example of the creativity that abounds in Timba vocal arranging. Instead of dividing the time equally between the coros and the lead singer's guías, the structure is asymmetrical -- each coro lasts 2.5 claves and is followed by a guía of only 1.5 claves.

There's no specific conga marcha for Coro 2. It's similar to Coro 1 once the marcha begins.

SECTION 13: MAMBO 2 (3:25 to 3:45): Mambo 1 consisted of a 2 bar phrase repeated 4 times, with the conga fill coming just after the beginning of the third repetition. Mambo 2, twice as long, is an example of the Timba arranging technique of combining coros and horns in the same section, with the horns answering an abbreviated version of Coro 2. Tomasito again plays his fill after the third phrase begins, and what a wicked fill it is! The one on the DVD, played about 5 years later, is even funkier than the one he recorded on the original on the CD (see next page for notation).

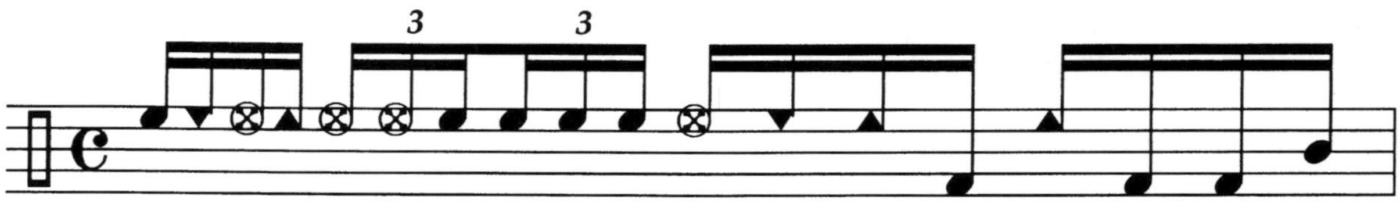

O B S T S S O O O O S B T O T O O O
L L R L R L R L R L R L L R L R R L

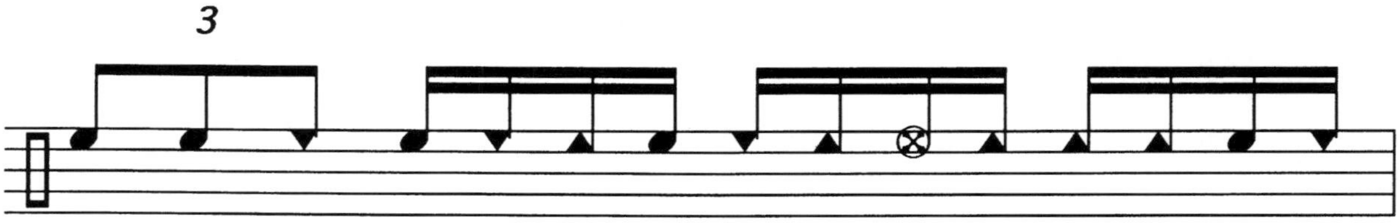

O O B O B T O B T S T T T O B
L R L R L L R L L R L R L R L

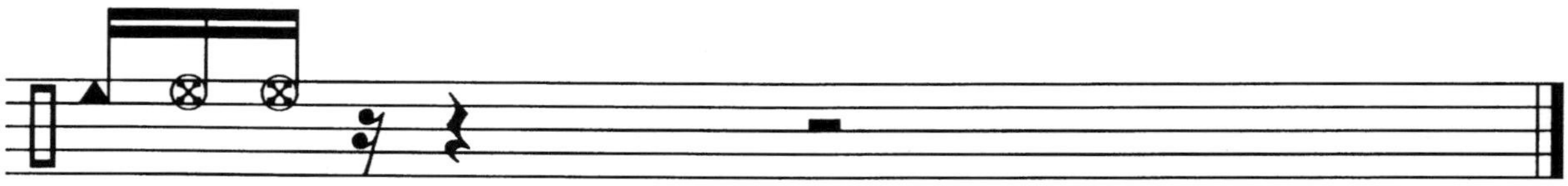

T S S
L R L

SECTION 14: BOMBA (within Mambo 2) (3:46 to 3:55): On the 3rd 4-bar phrase of Mambo 2 the rhythm section creates a uniquely Timba-esque rhythmic explosion by switching to Bomba while the mambo section is still in progress. The onset of the Bomba groove signals the dancers to break apart, raise their arms in the air and flaunt their *despelote* moves. The most obvious change in Bomba is made by the bassist, who begins sliding his hand down the lowest string, imitating the *Iyá* in certain *Batá* rhythms. The conguero has considerable freedom in his choice of marcha during the Bomba section as we've already seen. In this case, the basic pattern is:

B T S O O O T O B T S O T O O T
L L R L L R L R L L R L R L R L

The Bomba section ends on the same bloque as the earlier Pedal section:

SECTION 15: STILL MAMBO 2 (3:56 to 4:05): For the final 4 bars of the 16 bar mambo section, the rhythm section returns to a normal marcha, with Tomasito improvising several melodic variations and playing a fill into the next section.

SECTION 16: PEDAL – CORO 3 (4:06 to 4:25): Coro 3, like Coro 2, is introduced with a Pedal section, but this time it lasts twice as long. The mandatory bloques are shown here, and the conguero is free to fill the rests with harmonics or other tasteful improvisations.

On the second time through, Tomasito plays a crisp little fill and starts playing his Bomba marcha a bar early. The congas and drums almost always do this – as if to "rev up" the engine and let the dancers know that the Bomba is coming. The dancers would have already broken into *despelote* at the Pedal, but with the entrance of of the Bomba the more masterful among them would go into the *tembleque*, a uniquely Cuban dance move which defies all attempts at verbal description!

SECTION 17: BOMBA (STILL CORO 3) (4:26 to 4:46): As frequently happens, the rhythm section goes from Pedal to Bomba to a normal marcha, in that order, creating the effect of shifting through 3 different gears. On the DVD performance, Tomasito starts out with a variation of an earlier 3-drum marcha and then switches to a 2-drum pattern. If this second pattern sounds familiar to you, it's because it's essentially the same as a Bomba marcha we've already studied – Marcha #3 of Part 4 (DVD Chapters 10 & 11) – except that in this case it's used in a section that's in 2-3 clave so it starts in the middle of the phrase.

The section ends on the same bloque used to end the previous Bomba section. In the music of Paulito FG, and other Timba bands, it's common for a given arrangement to have one or more "signature" bloques which are repeated several times. In live performances of *No te lo creas,* which routinely run up to 15 minutes in length, many additional coros and mambos are added, sometimes on the spur of the moment, based on events in the nightclub on that particular night, resulting in many transitions in and out of Pedal, Bomba, Songo con Efectos, marcha, breakdown, and other gears – all cued with hand signals by the lead singer or musical director. As the song runs its course, its trademark bloques may be used many times. Other bands, such as Bamboleo, have generic bloques which are not linked to a specific arrangement and which can be mixed and matched, also using hand signals, to create variation from night to night on the same arrangement.

SECTION 18: MAMBO 3 (4:47 to 5:07): Same types of marcha variations as Mambo 2.

SECTION 19: BOMBA (5:07 to fade out): Still Mambo 3. Same treatment as Mambo 2.

PART 8: INVENTING YOUR OWN MARCHAS

For the final exercise in this course, we ask you to take everything you've learned and invent your own creative Timba marcha. Tomás composed an original bass and piano tumbao, which is played (audio only) in DVD Chapter 58. The idea of this exercise is for you to listen to the tumbaos over and over until they feel completely familiar and then to try to invent your marcha, just as you would in a Timba band if the arranger brought a new original song to rehearsal. **Don't watch DVD Chapter 59 until you've settled on your own pattern. Chapter 59 shows the marcha that Tomasito created to go with the same tumbao.**

Piano & Bass Tumbaos for Original Marcha - DVD Chapter 58 (audio only)

Clave: 2-3 Rumba
Tempo: 94

Tomasito's Marcha & Solo for the Exercise in Chpt 58 – DVD Chapter 59 (audio and video)

Clave: 2-3 Rumba
Tempo: 94

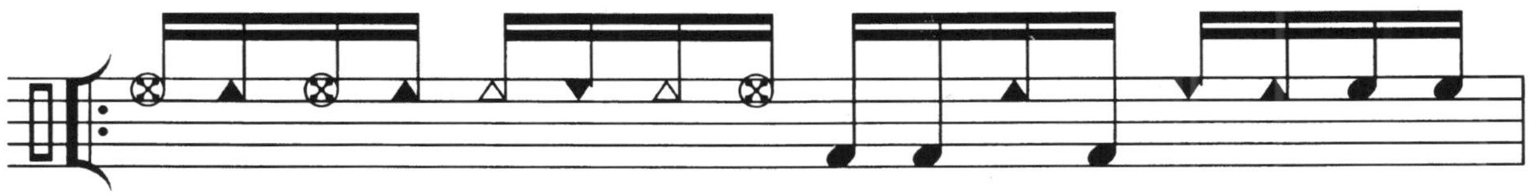

S T S T G B G S O O T O B T O O
R L R L R L R L R R L R L L R R

B T S T G S G O O O B O B O O B
L L R L R L R L R R L R L L R L

Soloing

At the end of DVD Chapter 59, Tomasito plays an extended solo creatively adapting the rudiments and recursos from Volumes I & II.

PART 9: EXERCISES IN 8TH NOTES

As explained earlier, we chose to write the body of the book in 16th notes, as most Cubans do, but we realize that many musicians in the United States and Europe are used to reading in 8ths. To make everyone happy we supply all the marchas in 8th notes here.

FROM PART 2:

DVD Chapter 1: 3-2 Rumba Clave

DVD Chapter 2: 2-3 Rumba Clave

DVD Chapter 3: 3-2 Son Clave

DVD Chapter 4: 2-3 Son Clave

FROM PART 4:

DVD Chapters 6 & 7: Step by Step Marcha #1

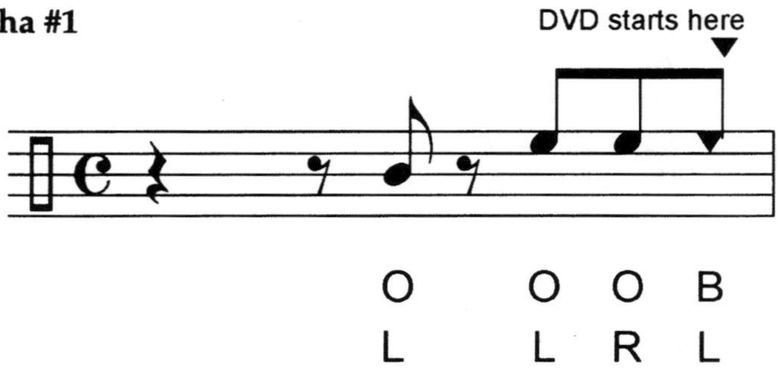

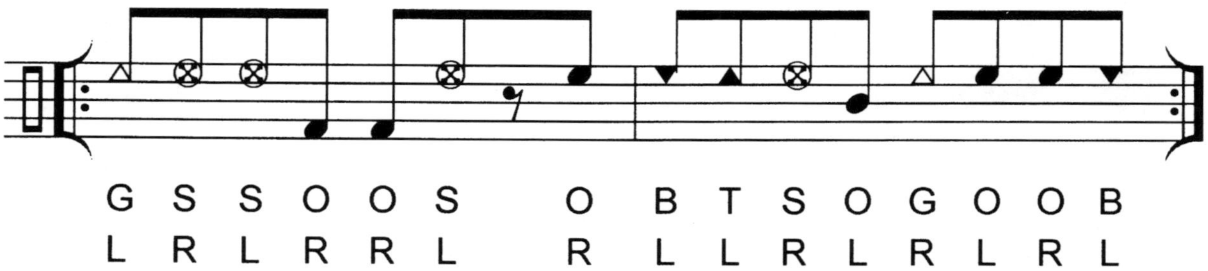

DVD Chapters 8 & 9: Step by Step Marcha #2

DVD Chapters 10 & 11: Step by Step Marcha #3

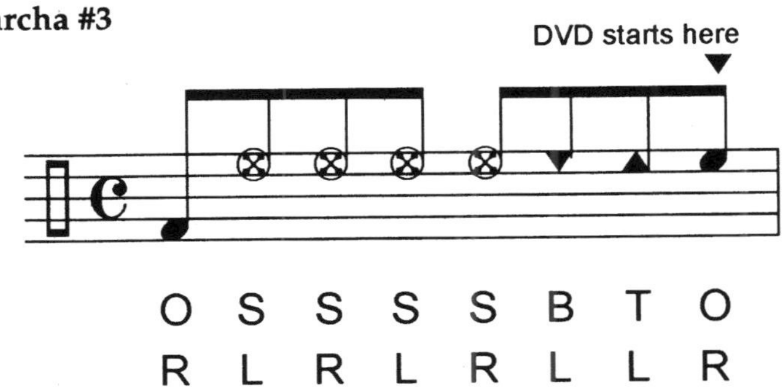

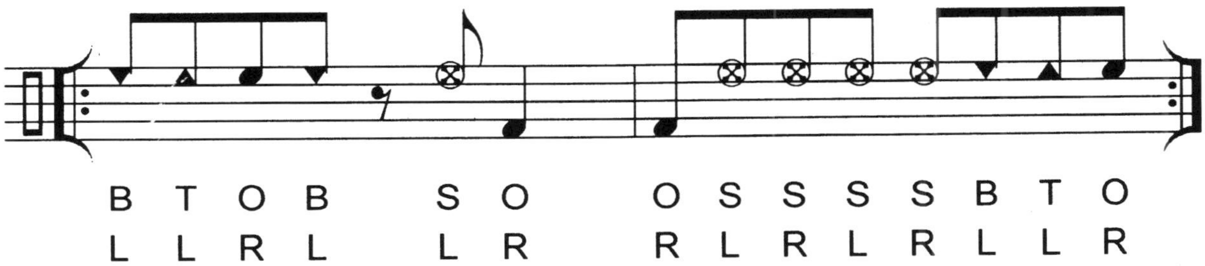

DVD Chapters 12 & 13: Step by Step Marcha #4

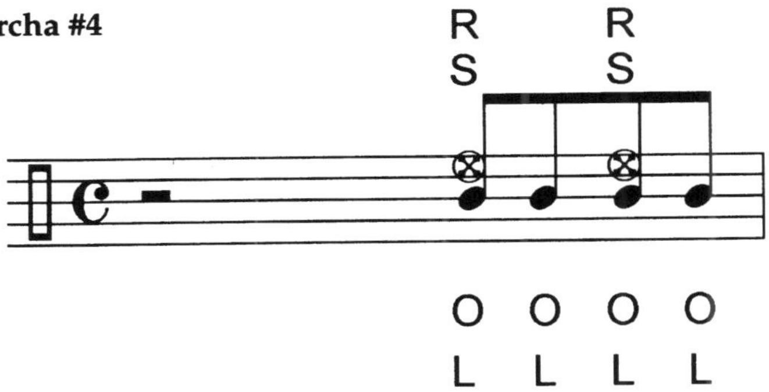

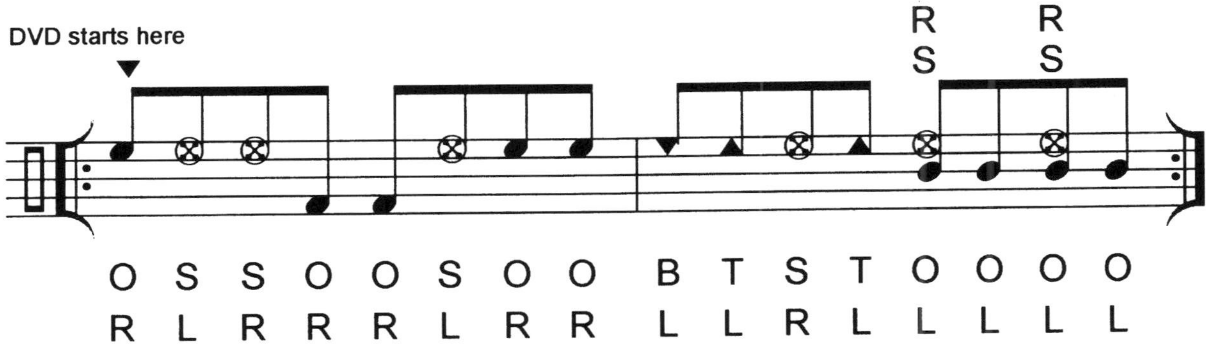

DVD Chapters 14 & 15: Step by Step Marcha #5

O S S O O O S

R L R L R L L

S O BG O BG S O T O S S O O O S

R L R L R L R L R L R L R L L

*= Bass Ghost

DVD Chapters 16 & 17: Step by Step Marcha #6

O S S O O O B

R L R L R L L

T S T S B T O T O S S O O O B

L R L R L L R L R L R L R L L

DVD Chapters 18 & 19: Step by Step Marcha #7

B T S O/S O O M M M B S G O O O
L L L L/R R R L R L L R R L L R

DVD Chapters 20 & 21: Step by Step Marcha #8

DVD starts here

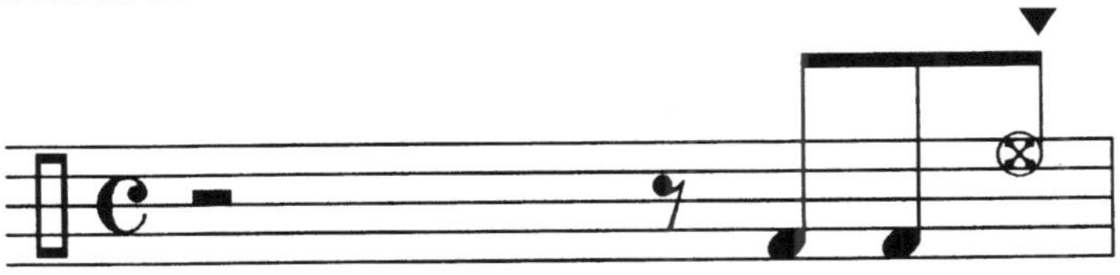

O O S
R R L

S
R

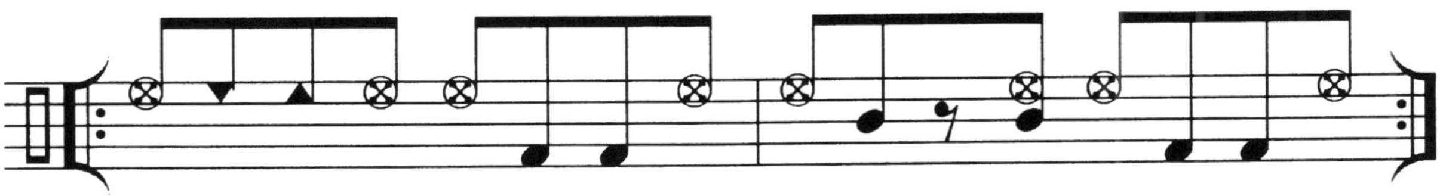

S B T S S O O S S O O S O O S
R L L R L R R L R L L L R R L

DVD Chapters 22 & 23: Step by Step Marcha #9

DVD starts here

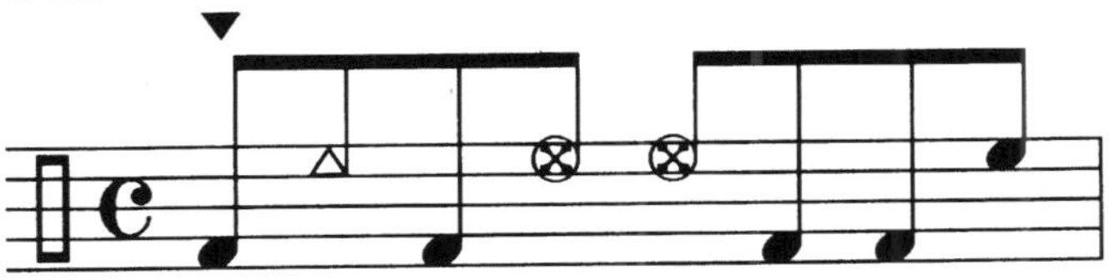

O G O S S O O O
R L R R L R R L

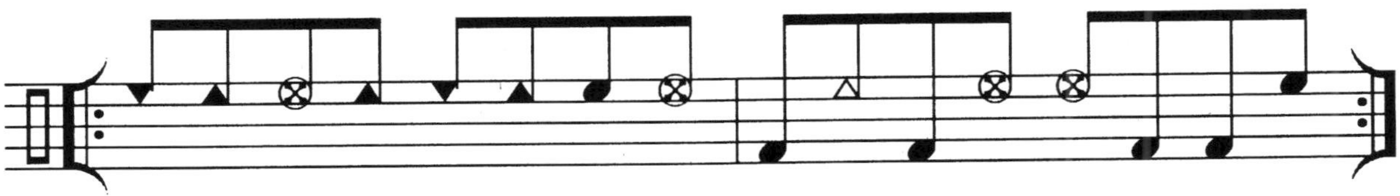

B T S T B T O S O G O S S O O O
L L R L L L R L R L R R L R R L

DVD Chapters 24 & 25: Step by Step Marcha #10

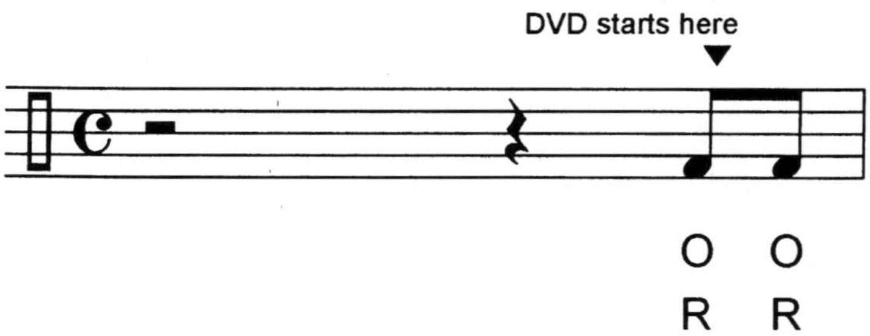

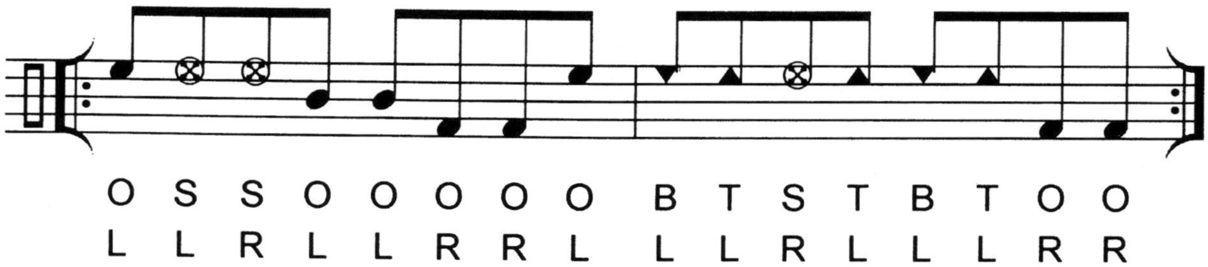

DVD Chapters 26 & 27: Step by Step Marcha #11

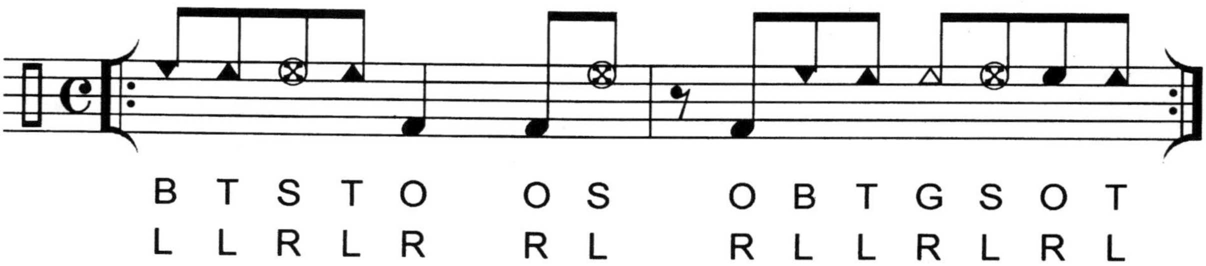

FROM PART 5:

DVD Chapters 28 & 29: Longer Marcha #1

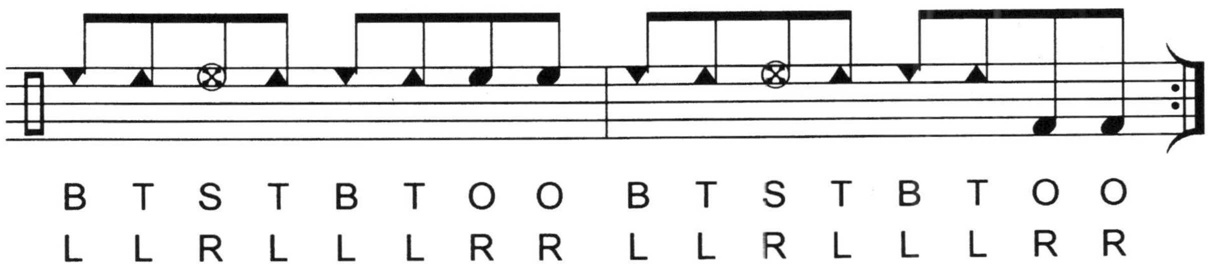

DVD Chapters 30 & 31: Longer Marcha #2

B T S G O O G B T S T B T O B
L L R R L L R L L R L L L R L

T O S O O S O O B T S T B T O T
L R L R R L R R L L R L L L R L

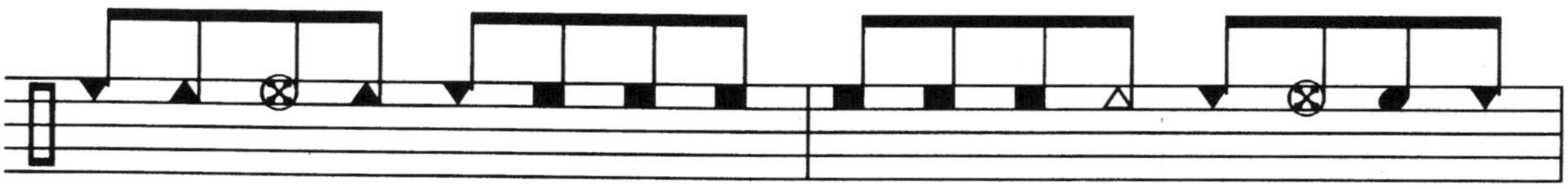

B T S T B M M M M M M G B S O B
L L R L L R L R L R L R L L R L

T O S O O S O O B T S T B T O T
L R L R R L R R L L R L L L R L

DVD Chapters 32 & 33: Longer Marcha #3

DVD Chapters 34 & 35: Longer Marcha #4

O
R

B T S T G S O S O O G O T B T O
L L R L R L R L R L R L R L L R

B T S T G S O S O G O G S O
L L R L R L R L R L R R L R

DVD Chapters 36 & 37: Longer Marcha #5

O O B T G S O S O O G O T B T O
L R L L R L R L R L R L R L L R

B T S T G S O S O G O G O S O O
L L R L R L R L R L R L R L R R

DVD Chapters 38 & 39: Longer Marcha #6

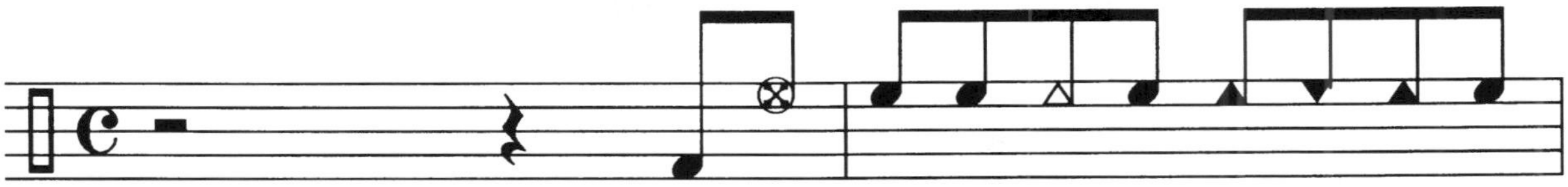

O S O O G O T B T O
R L R L R L R L L R

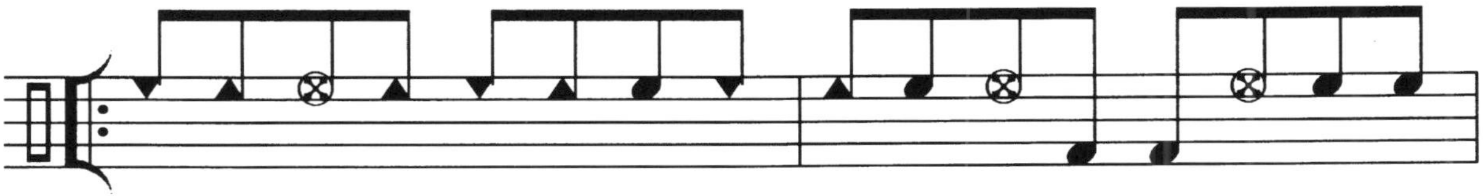

B T S T B T O B T O S O O S O O
L L R L L L R L L R L R R L R R

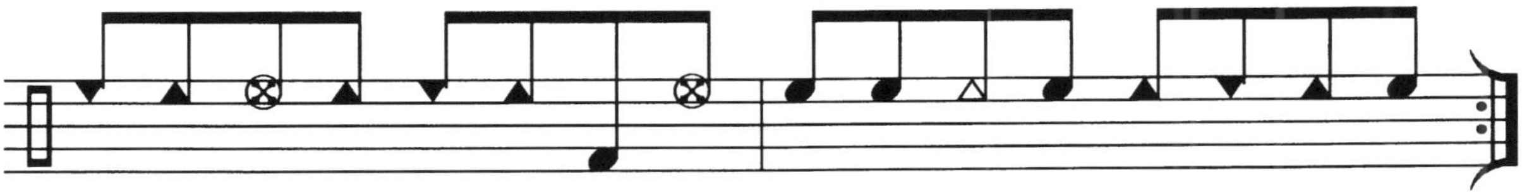

B T S T B T O S O O G O T B T O
L L R L L L R L R L R L R L L R

DVD Chapters 40 & 41: Longer Marcha #7

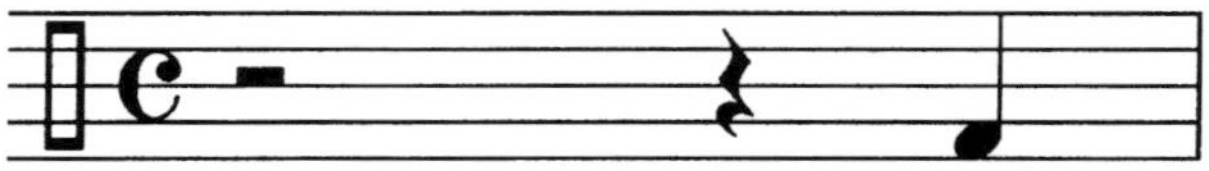

O
R

S O B T G S O B T S T G S O B
L R L L R L R L L R L R L R L

T O S O O S O B T S T S O
L R L R R L R L L R L L R

DVD Chapters 42 & 43: Longer Marcha #8

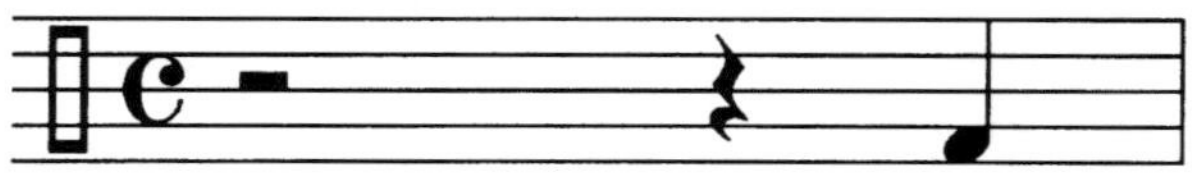

O
R

O O B T G S O B T S T G S O B
R R L L R L R L L R L R L R L

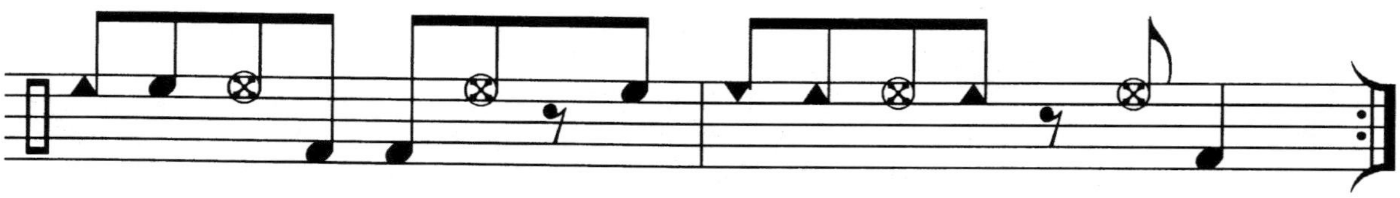

T O S O O S O B T S T S O
L R L R R L R L L R L L R

DVD Chapters 44 & 45: Longer Marcha #9

B T S T O B T O B T S T B T O B
L L R L R L L R L L R L L L R L

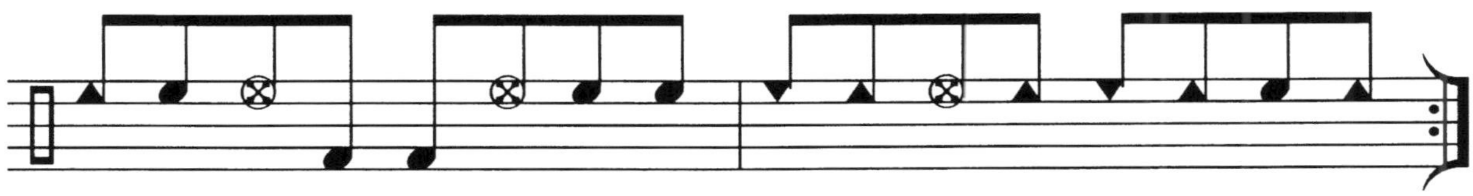

T O S O O D O O B T S T B T O T
L R L R R L R R L L R L L L R L

DVD Chapters 46 & 47: Longer Marcha #10

O S
R L

O O S O O S O O B T S T B M M M
R R L R R L R R L L R L L L R L

B S T O O S O O B T S T B T O S
L R L R R L R R L L R L L L R L

FROM PART 6:

DVD Chapter 48: Pedal Entrance #1

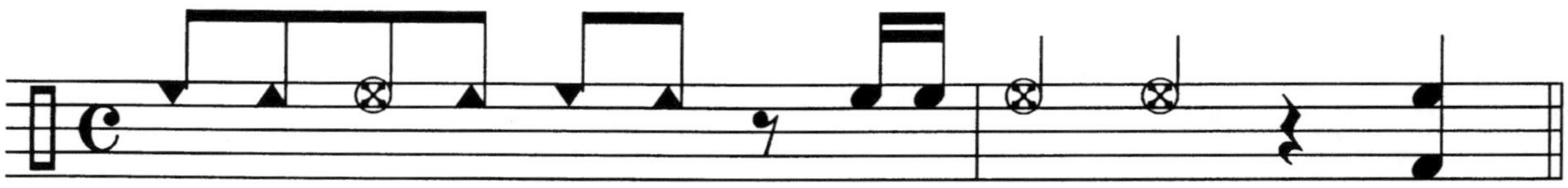

B T S T B T OO S S O/O

L L R L L L RL R L R/L

Pedal Section

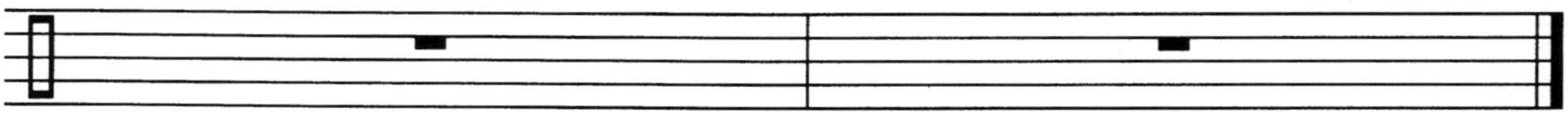

DVD Chapter 49: Pedal Entrance #2

B T S T B T OO S S O/O

L L R L L L RL R L R/L

Pedal Section

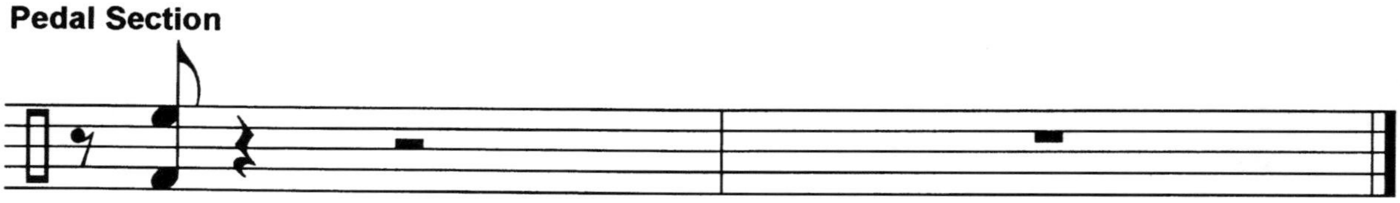

O/O

R/L

DVD Chapter 50: Pedal Entrance #3

B T S T B T O O S S O/O
L L R L L L R L R L R/L

Pedal Section

O/O O O O
R/L R R L

DVD Chapter 51: Pedal Entrance #4

B T S T B T O O O O O O S S O O
L L R L L L R L R L R L R L R L

Pedal Section

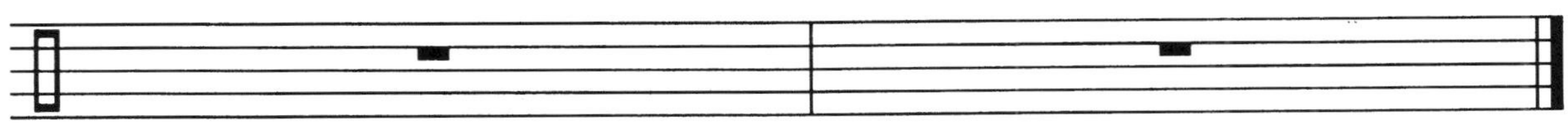

DVD Chapter 52: Pedal Entrance #5

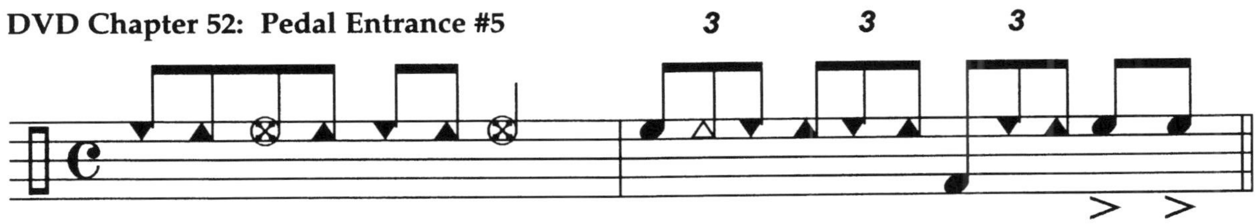

B T S T B T S O G B T B T O B T O O
L L R L L L R R L R R L L R L L R L

Pedal Section

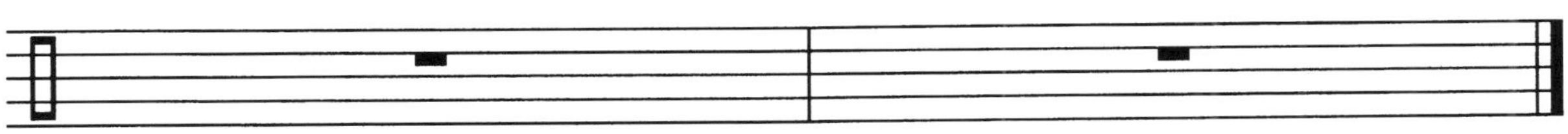

DVD Chapter 53: Pedal Entrance #6

B T S T B T O O B T S T O B T S

L L R L L L R R L L R L R L L R

Pedal Section

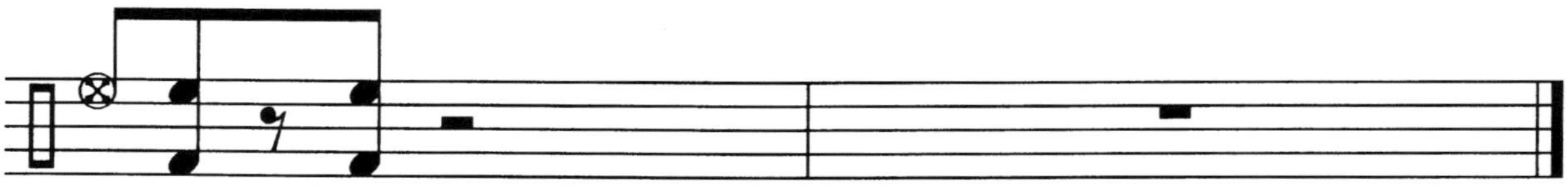

S O/O O/O

L L/R L/R

DVD Chapter 54: Pedal Improvisation #1

Pedal Section

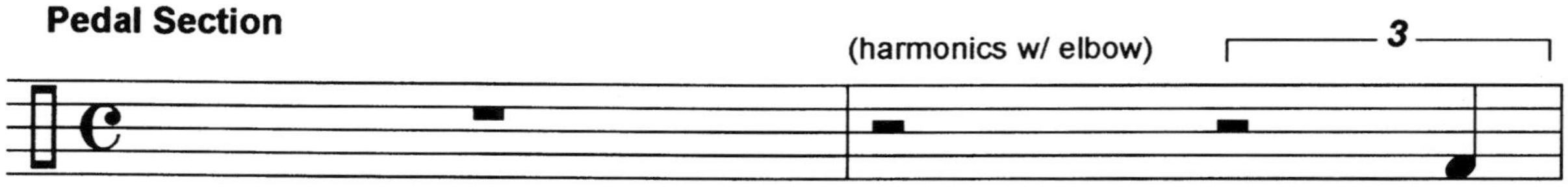

H

R

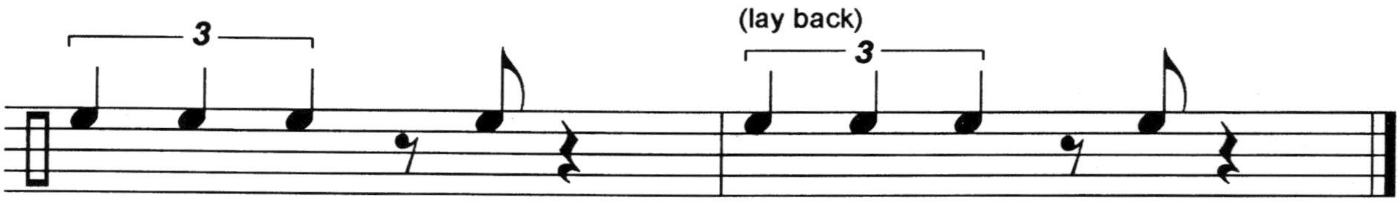

H H H H H H H H

R R R R R R R R

DVD Chapter 55: Pedal Improvisation #2

(harmonics w/ elbow)

H H H H H H H H

R R R R R R R R

DVD Chapter 56: Complete Pedal Section

O S S O O O O O B T S T B T O O
L L R L L R R L L L R L L L R R

last time

O S S O O O O O B T S T O B T S
L L R L L R R L L L R L R L L R

Pedal Section

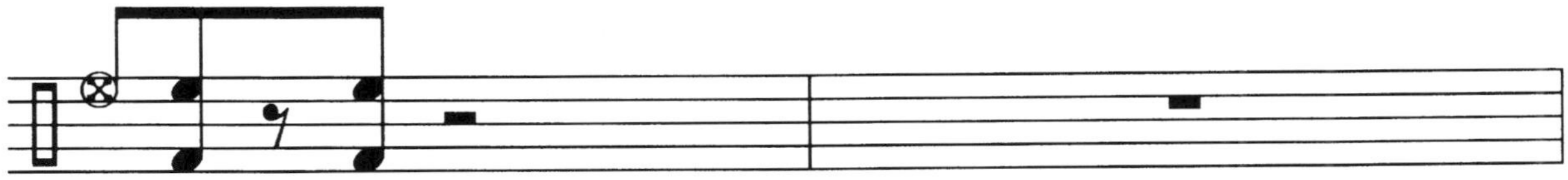

S O/O O/O
L R/L R/L

O O O B O/O
R L R R R/L

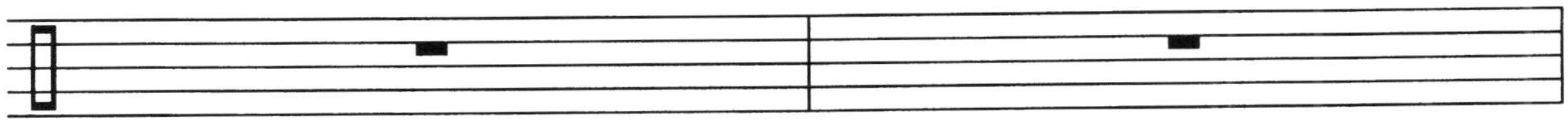

Into Next Marcha Section

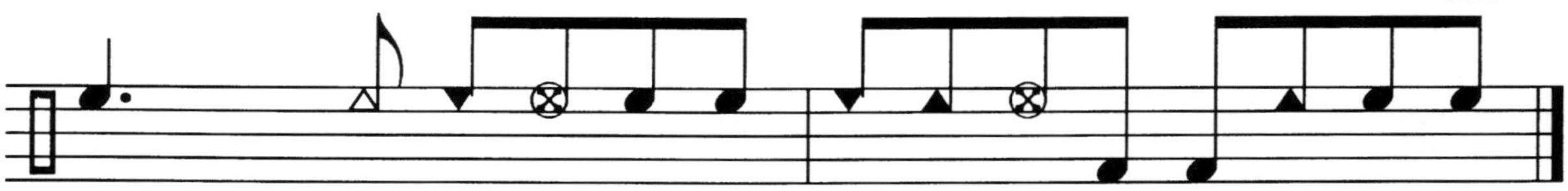

FROM PART 7:

SECTION 1: INTRODUCTION (0:00 to 0:11):

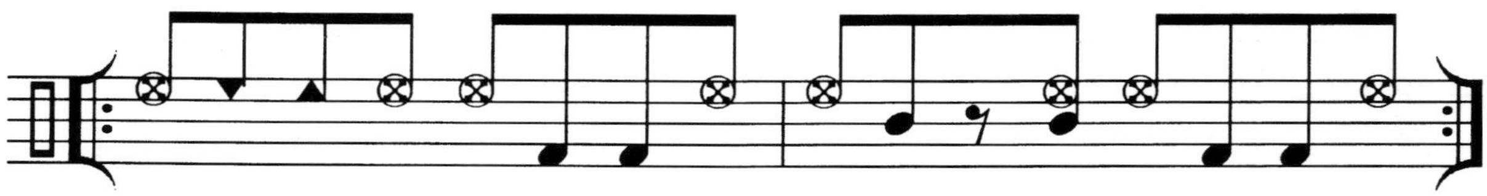

SECTION 2: CUERPO A (0:12 to 0:31): basic marcha:

Cuerpo A -- Variation #1

B T S T B T O O B T S T O S O O

L L R L L L R R L L R L R L R R

Cuerpo A -- Variation #2

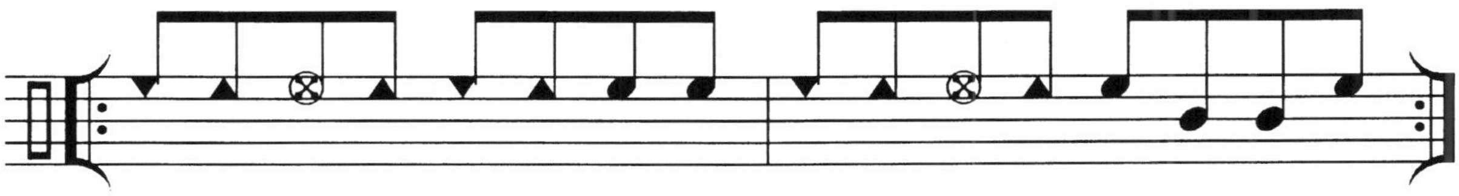

B T S T B T O O B T S T O O O O

L L R L L L R R L L R L R L L R

Cuerpo A -- Variation #3

B T S T B T O O T B S T B T O O

L L R L L L R L R L R L L L R R

Cuerpo A -- Variation #4

B T S T O O O O B T S T O S O O

L L R L R L L R L L R L R L R R

SECTION 3: CUERPO B – (0:32 to 0:51):

B T S T B T O S O G O S S O O O
L L R L L L R L R L R R L R R L

SECTION 4: REPEAT OF INTRO (0:51 to 0:56): (like Section 1)

SECTION 5: CUERPO A2 (2nd time) (0:57 to 1:17): (like Section 2)

SECTION 6: CUERPO B2 (2nd time): (like Section 3)

SECTION 7: PUENTE ("bridge") (1:37 to 1:42):

end of Cuerpo B

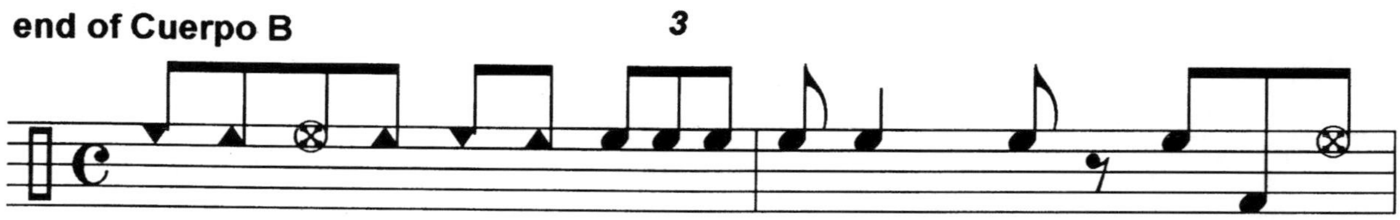

B T S T B T O O O O O O O O S
L L R L L L R L L R L R L R L

Puente

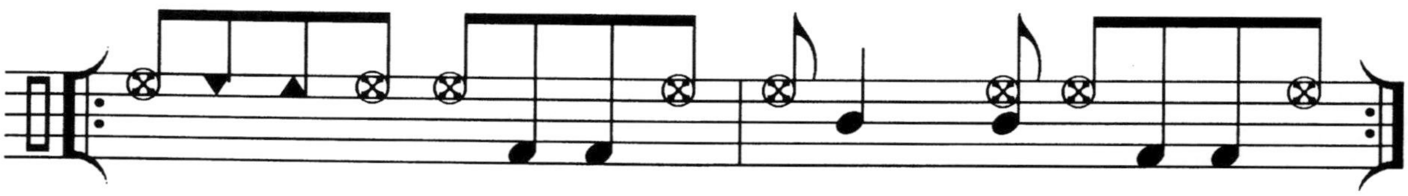

S B T S S O O S S O O/S S O O S
R L L R L R R L R L L/R L R R L

SECTION 8: PIANO TUMBAO (1:43 to 1:53):

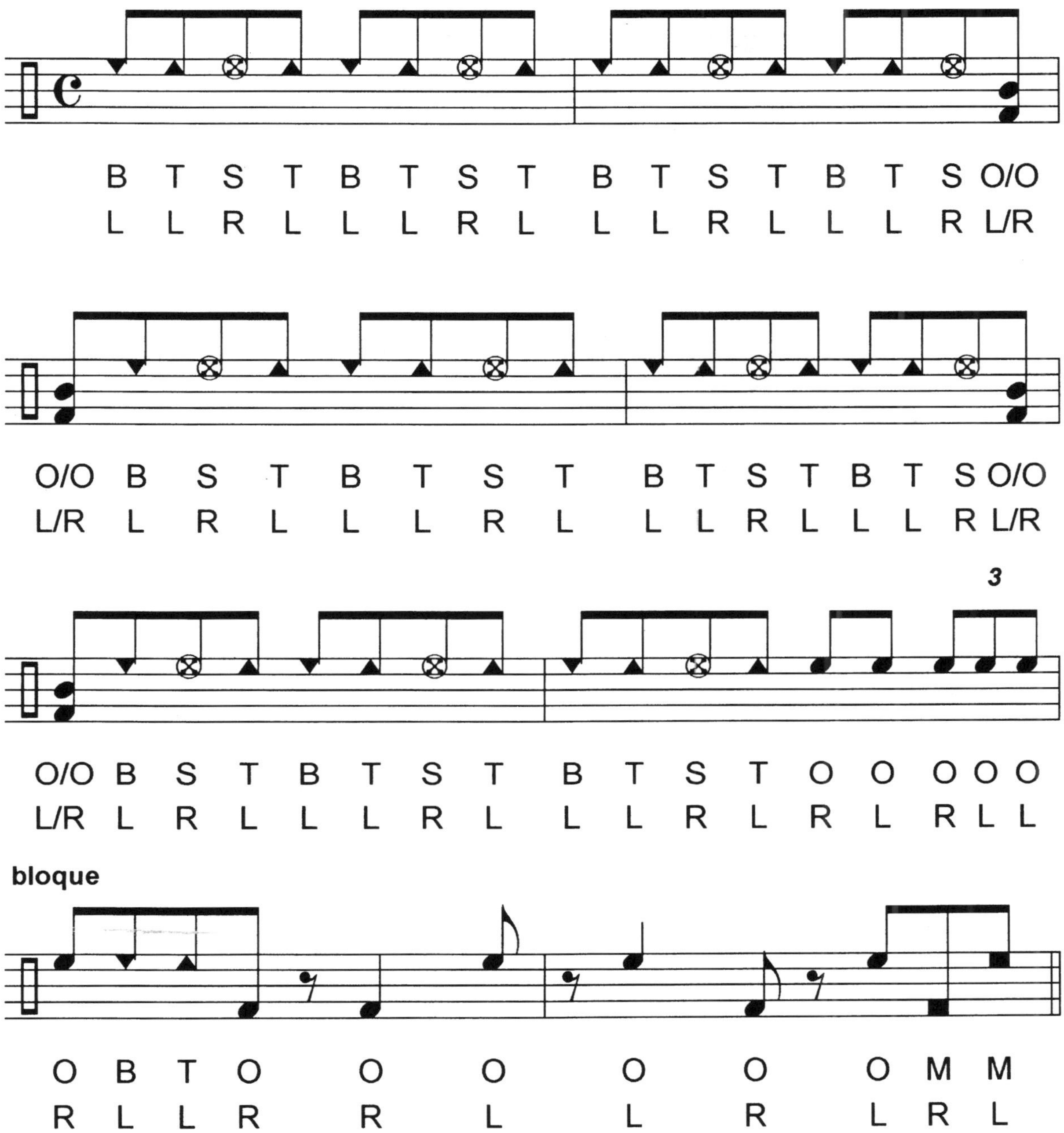

SECTION 9: MONTUNO 1 – CORO 1 (1:54 to 2:33):

SECTION 9: 2nd example:

SECTION 10: MAMBO 1 (2:34 to 2:53):

O S S O O O O O B T S T G S O B
R L R L L R R L R L R L R L R L

T O S O O S O O B T S T G S G S
L R L R R L R R L L R L R L R L

SECTION 10 - 2nd example: SOLO (2:45):

O B S S S B T B T S S
L L R R L R L R L R L

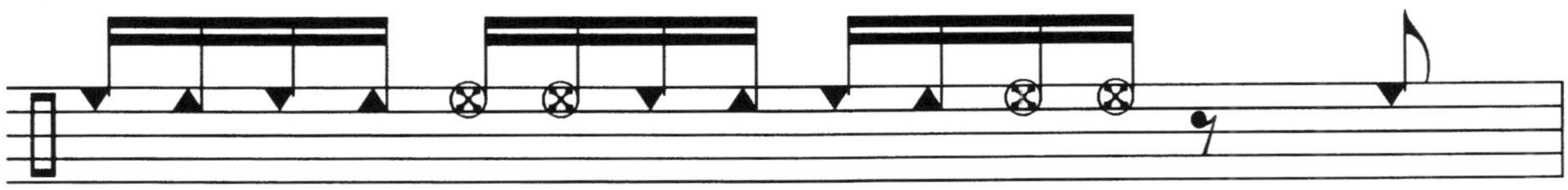

B T B T S S B T B T S S B
R L R L R L R L R L R L R

return to marcha

S B T O O O G B
R L L R R L R L

SECTION 11: CORO 2/PEDAL (2:54 to 3:04):

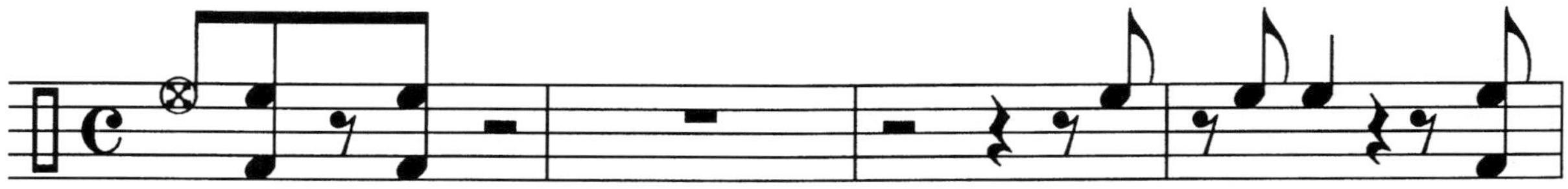

S O/O O/O O O O O/O
L R/L R/L R L R R/L

O O O O O S O
R R L L R L R

SECTION 12: MONTUNO 2 – CONTINUATION OF CORO 2 (3:05 to 3:24): (no example)

SECTION 13: MAMBO 2 (3:25 to 3:45): SOLO

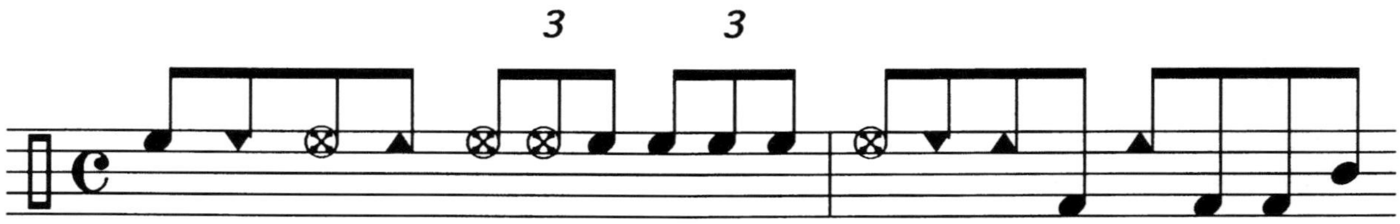

O B S T S S O O O O S B T O T O O O
L L R L R L R L R L R L L R L R R L

O O B O B T O B T S T T T O B
L R L R L L R L L R L R L R L

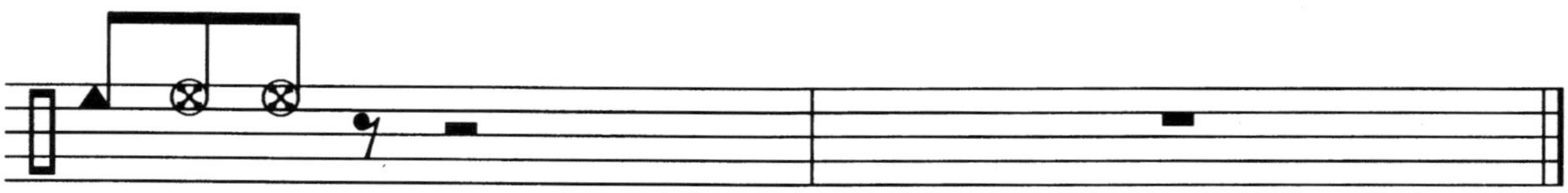

T S S
L R L

SECTION 14: BOMBA (within Mambo 2) (3:46 to 3:55):

B T S O O O T O B T S O T O O T

L L R L L R L R L L R L R L R L

SECTION 15: STILL MAMBO 2 (3:56 to 4:05): (no example)

SECTION 16: PEDAL – CORO 3 (4:06 to 4:25):

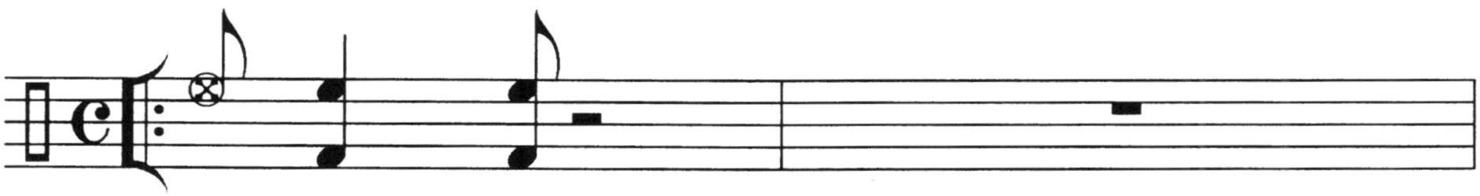

S O/O O/O

L R/L R/L

O O O O/O

R L R R/L

SECTION 17: BOMBA (STILL CORO 3) (4:26 to 4:46):

O

R

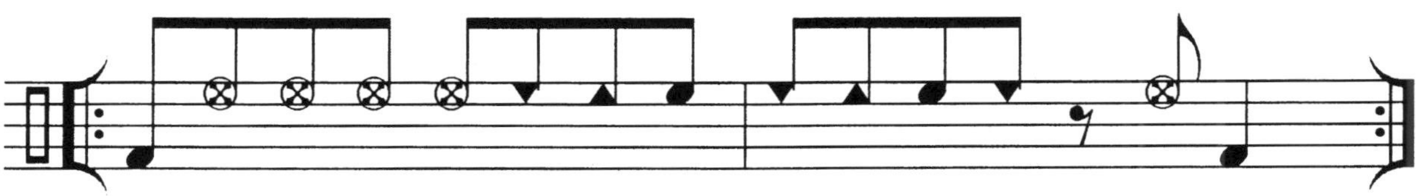

O S S S S B T O B T O B S O

R L R L R L L R L L R L L R

SECTION 18: MAMBO 3 (4:47 to 5:07): .

SECTION 19: BOMBA (5:07 to fade out):

FROM PART 8:

DVD Chapter 58: Original Tumbao (no conga – audio only)

DVD Chapter 59: Tomasito's Marcha for Original Tumbao

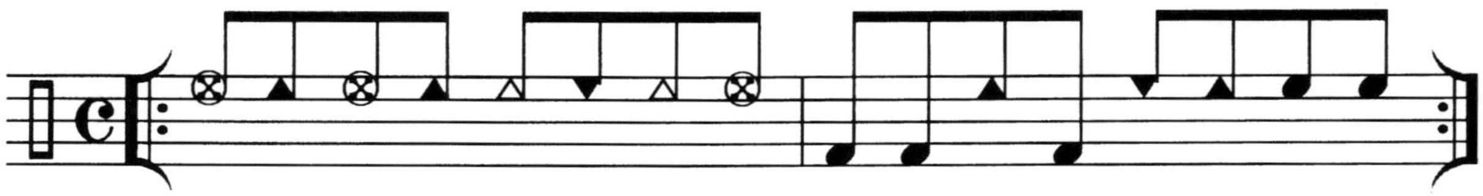

S T S T G B G S O O T O B T O O

R L R L R L R L R R L R L L R R

B T S T G S G O O O B O B O O B

L L R L R L R L R R L R L L R L